LET GO

MATT MIOFSKY

LET

GO

LEANING INTO THE FUTURE
WITHOUT FEAR

ABINGDON PRESS

NASHVILLE

LET GO
LEANING INTO THE FUTURE WITHOUT FEAR

Copyright © 2019 by Abingdon Press

Library of Congress Cataloging-in-Publication Data has been requested.

ISBN 978-1-5018-7962-3

19 20 21 22 23 24 25 26 27 28—10 9 8 7 6 5 4 3 2 1
MANUFACTURED IN THE UNITED STATES OF AMERICA

To my wife, Jessica. We have changed a lot over twenty years of marriage and managed it well. Here is to keeping it up for all the change God has in store for us.

CONTENTS

—⁓—

INTRODUCTION

—◦◦◦—

Y ou don't have to do it alone. That is the first thing that
I want you to hear. And before I even explain what
"it" is, know this: you aren't alone in what you might be
going through right now, and you don't have to navigate
the uncertainty of your life all by yourself. Maybe right now
you are in the midst of major change, and you are scared
about what it will bring. Maybe you are contemplating
a change and aren't sure how to weigh the risk involved.
Maybe you are on the other side of change and now are
secretly scared of doing anything to screw up what feels like
a stable life. But here is the thing: we cannot always control
change. It happens. There is no avoiding it. Just when you
think things in your life are stable, and you are trying like
hell to keep it that way, the rug can be pulled out from under
you. Whatever you are facing right now, whatever changes
are happening in your life, or whatever fears you secretly
harbor, you are not alone.

This book is a guide to managing the transitions in your
life using faith as your compass.

It is often said that change is part of life, and it's true.
But there is a difference between change and transition.
While change may be a given, transition is not. William
Bridges made this observation in a book entitled *Managing
Transitions*, written for corporations and organizations
that undergo major change. That book contributed to a

burgeoning field within business called change management. The essence of the insight was simple. Change, on the one hand, is an external and physical evolution, manipulation, or development that happens within an organization. Some changes are intentional and controlled by the leaders of the organization. Other changes cannot be controlled. Either way, change is always happening all around us, on a personal, organizational, civic, political, or global level. Things are changing. Always.

Change management is the art of ushering in intentional change (or dealing with unintentional change) by tending to the transitions that must happen in and with the very people who are experiencing those changes.

Transition, on the other hand, is an internal, psychological process that happens on the personal level. Transition is about what is happening to people, in people, and with people as they *experience* change. Unlike the change itself, transition is not a given. By definition, transition means moving from one place or situation to another. But not everyone makes it successfully to that other place. Successful transition requires effort, care, and intentionality. People can learn to internalize and transition along with the changes that happen around them. They can also choose *not* to, which usually results in getting stuck. I suspect all of us can call to mind people in our company, organization, or church who simply refuse to accept, process, or adapt to changes that are happening all around them. Circumstances, processes, or realities may change, but they don't (and often won't!). They refuse to move forward, and very often they get left behind or become an impediment to the organization. Therefore, change management is the art of ushering in intentional change (or dealing with unintentional change) by tending to the transitions that must happen in and with the very people who are experiencing those changes. People who ignore the need for change management do so at their own peril.

So with this distinction in mind, let me say it again. Change is an unavoidable part of life, but transition is not. To take this a bit further, change is easy. Despite what everyone says, it is simple to change things. Transitions, however, are hard. Most of us find this out the hard way.

Take a church, for instance (I am a pastor, so you'll get a few church references along the way in this book). Suppose a new pastor begins working at a one-hundred-year-old church steeped in traditions and ways of doing things that people have gotten used to. Take something simple, like the time of the church's worship service. Imagine that for one hundred years, worship has started at 10:00 a.m. For the hour before worship, the church gathers for Sunday school (for you non-church people, these are small groups that pray and study the Bible. Think of it as a religious book group).

For the thirty minutes after worship, church members usually gather for coffee, donuts, and gossip. Factor in travel time, and you have a group of people who have a very regular, two-and-a-half-hour routine every Sunday morning. And for some people, they have been doing this their entire life. So much so that it has become a rhythm, likely leading to other traditions. Maybe they go to lunch after worship. That will get them to the restaurant just before noon (in time to beat the other churches in the area). This is their life, and they rather like it that way. That is, after all, why they have done it for all these years.

Now suppose this new pastor comes in and within the first month realizes that the church really needs to have two worship services because younger generations aren't connecting with the traditional style of the 10:00 a.m. service. So she decides to begin a second service. To accommodate the new service, she changes the times, but only slightly. Now there will be an 8:30 a.m. service and a 10:30 a.m. service. That way, there is still time in between for Sunday school, and people can maintain the tradition of donuts and gossip after church. It will work great, and it isn't that big of a change. The longtime members will have to adjust by only thirty minutes. It seems simple and makes perfect sense to the pastor. So the next weekend she stands up in church and announces that, beginning in a month, worship times will change to accommodate a new worship. Boom! It took her less than a week to change something that had been in place for one hundred years. And it was easy! All she had to do was, well, change it. What is all the fuss about?

She gets her answer immediately after church is over. During the coffee hour, she is inundated with people who are confused, surprised, and upset by the change. They bring up all sorts of collateral changes and unintended consequences that the pastor didn't expect (after all, thirty minutes is a big deal when you are trying to beat the church across town to lunch). But more than all of that, there is all this *emotion* that the pastor wasn't prepared for. Even after explaining, showing the rationale, and making a very reasonable and logical case for the changes, she finds that the people aren't budging. That is because the change may have happened, but the transition hasn't even begun. In order for the church to successfully manage a simple change, like the time of worship, there is going to need to be a long, intentional, and very careful process of managing transition for people. Just ask any pastor who has done this (or failed in the attempt). He or she will tell you that the change may be instant, but even a simple transition like this can take years.

Learning how to manage change and transition in our personal lives is critically important if we are to become the people we were created to be.

So you get the difference. Change versus transition. We get change management on the organizational level, and there are plenty of resources, exercises, and books out there to teach leaders how to do this. But what does all that have to do with our personal lives? That is what I spent a lot of my ministry thinking about. What I have discovered is that this same dynamic between change and transition is true in our individual lives. And yet there are fewer resources exploring this on a personal level than there are for people in business. We assume that people will figure out how to change in their personal lives. If they want to lose weight, they can change their eating habits and exercise more. If you are unhappy in a relationship, change your partner or spouse. If you don't like what a particular habit is doing to you, change your behavior. If you don't like your job, change your job—or maybe even your career pathway. If you don't like where you live, change locations or cities. If your friends are boring and shallow, change your friendship circle. If you feel stuck and don't like the direction your life seems to be going, change directions. It seems pretty easy. If you want your life to look different, then change it.

And here's the thing. Change is actually pretty easy. We can find a new job. We can break up with our boyfriend or girlfriend. We can stop hanging out with certain people and start hanging out with others. We can wake up earlier, start working out, or decide to change careers. We can read a new book or take up a new hobby. We can change things in our life. Change is easy. But what many of us find is that the changes we try to make don't actually solve our underlying sense of dissatisfaction that led us to the change. We don't feel any different, we don't act particularly different, and all too quickly we can return to what feels like the old normal, even though where we live, who we are with, and what we do for a living all have been changed. We can make changes to the circumstances of our life, but transitioning who we are, how we think, and what we are capable of is much harder work. We can change what we do, but the internal and deeply personal work of changing *who we are* is hard. Most of us don't know how to do it, and then we try to do it alone, without the wisdom and help of others or of the God who created us.

That is why I wrote this book. I believe that learning how to manage change and transition in our personal lives is critically important if we are to become the people we were created to be and to live the lives we were created to live. For that reason, managing change and transition in our lives is not only personal or psychological work but also spiritual work. If you are Jesus's follower, then change and transition are part of the package. I mean, Jesus was pretty explicit about his intentions. He doesn't want to tweak a few things in your life. Jesus wants to transform you. The Bible is crystal clear about what following Christ means: "This means that anyone who belongs to Christ has become a new person. The old life is gone; a new life has begun!" (2 Corinthians 5:17 NLT).

We follow a God who wants to change our lives, who doesn't want us to be the same people tomorrow that we are today. That means that learning how to manage change and transition is critically important to a healthy faith. Some of you right now are facing major changes in your life, such as divorce, job loss, depression, parenting, aging, addiction, restlessness, graduation, retirement, failure, success, a new city, the loss of someone you love, starting a new business, or calling it quits on a failed attempt at something new. Changes are all around us. In the midst of them you may feel alone, but you are not. You don't have to manage change alone. We can do this together. More important, God is right alongside you preparing a future for you that you may not be able to feel or see right now.

So this book is about the changes life throws at us or that we choose for ourselves. It is a guide on how to manage those changes and transitions in a faithful and healthy way—not alone, but together with a God who is guiding us.

Anytime we talk about change, we have to confront the greatest obstacle to making this journey from here to there. The greatest obstacle is not time, money, the right job, or a lack of resources. It is not a lack of knowledge or experience. The greatest obstacle to navigating change in your life is fear.

I am writing this introduction during the week leading up to Christmas. If you read the Christmas story, there are no fewer than four references to fear. The first reaction people had to the good news that God wanted to change their lives, and the world, was fear! So when the angel showed up to Zechariah (John the Baptist's father), Joseph, Mary, and the shepherds in the fields, some of the first words they spoke were, "Do not be afraid." Fear, it seems, is the natural reaction even to good news and answered prayers. It is our default response to change. Even when we human beings are about to get what we want, we still can't help but be afraid!

And it doesn't stop there. Throughout his ministry Jesus continually had to address the fear that his disciples were constantly battling. When Jesus appeared to his followers after his resurrection, his first words to them were the same: "Don't be afraid."

The story of our life with God starts with God addressing our fears. Fear is the enemy that will keep you from becoming the person that God wants you to be and living the life that God wants you to live. And nothing brings out our fears more than change! So change and fear go hand in hand. In learning how to manage change and transition, a natural part of faith must include also confronting not just our individual fears but also the idea of fear itself.

But managing transition and overcoming fear in life do not happen in an instant. There are no magic bullets and no ways to skip over the hard stuff. This is a journey that each of us has to travel. Fortunately, we are not left to our own devices as we start this journey. The Bible doesn't just have stories and examples of what the journey looks like; it has a road map. Through the experiences of those who came before us, the Bible teaches us what managing change and facing fear looks like and how to do it alongside the God who will lead us.

There are a lot of stories we could focus on, but we are going to use one of the most significant stories in the Bible. It is *the* most significant story in the Old Testament: the exodus story. The exodus is a literal journey that the Israelites took from the land of Egypt, through the wilderness, and to the "promised land." But the exodus story is much more than that. It is also a journey that the Israelites had to take from being the people they were to becoming the people God wanted them to be. It was a journey from slavery to freedom and a journey from forgotten people to chosen people. The exodus story is a journey of becoming someone new so that you can live in a new way and discover a new vision for life and purpose for existing. The exodus story is a holistic story of managing change and transition at every level—literal, geographical, psychological, emotional, and spiritual. In this way the exodus story is more than a historical account of a certain group of people some 3,500 years ago. It is also an archetype of all of our stories. It is a roadmap for how change looks when you are following God's lead. It is the story from which all the other stories of the Bible build. Even Jesus himself saw his life and ministry as a fulfilment of this original story of transformation.

So whether you are reacting to a change you didn't choose, are contemplating a new reality for your life, or are in the midst of answering a God-inspired call to step away from where you are and toward something new, you are in the right place. Some of you are facing personal change and transition. Others of you may be leading in a church, company, or organization. Some of you are trying to navigate change with and for your family or a group of people you love. This book will give you plenty to think about, no matter at what level you find yourself managing change.

Wherever you are, just know that you aren't alone. We are going to do this together. And if you are scared, that is normal. It is more than that: it is good. It is a sign that you are doing something significant or following God in a truly courageous way. People have always been scared right before God does something new and incredible in their life. So take that fear as a good sign—even rejoice in it. But don't give in to it, and don't listen to it. Ultimately, your fear is the only thing standing in the way. It is the only obstacle between where you are and where God wants to lead you. It is the only real thing blocking you from transitioning from who you are to the person God wants you to be. So we will deal with fear, we will learn how to navigate through it, and ultimately, we will learn that, with God, fear doesn't have to win. We will conquer fear, and we will step out. We will navigate this change and transition, and we will be the better because we were willing to go for it. So as we set out on the journey, give yourself grace. Remember that it is a process. And, most important, know that you aren't alone. You have a God who is leading you every step of the way.

Chapter 1

GO FOR IT

—◦◦◦—

You should go for it.

If there is something you have been thinking about trying, a risk you've been considering, a change that you want to make, or a new endeavor that you want to go for, you should do it. I know it isn't that easy. There are real-world considerations. You have to think about what could go wrong. You have to consider the timing. Where are you going to get the money? What happens if it doesn't work? Is the change you want to make a smart one? Is it a God-inspired change or just something that is fundamentally selfish? What resources are you going to need to accomplish it? Are you moving too fast, or is the change too abrupt?

It is good to ask those questions. You have to think about what you are doing. Rash change is rarely good change. You have to count the costs and consider the risks. That is part of any new adventure. But let's assume you've done that. You have vetted your plan by God, by people you love and trust, and you've adapted to feedback and planned for the unknown. You've prayed about it. But after all the vetting and talking and considering and praying, there is still risk. There is still uncertainty. You still aren't sure. I get it. Really. And that is why I will say it again.

You should go for it.

Why? Because you were made for this.

Made for what, exactly?

You were made to take risks, to overcome challenges, and to conquer fears.

You were made to move, to change, and to grow. You aren't the first one to be scared. And you won't be the last one. There is help for how to do this. That is what this book is about.

The Bible is a story about how God moved among God's people in history. But it is more than that. It is also a template for how God still moves among people today. When we read stories in the scripture, we are, in a way, reading stories about us. And if there is one *type* of story that is told over and over again, it is migration stories, traveling stories, journeys in which God takes a person or a group of people from one place to another. One of the first people we meet in the Bible, Abram, is an old man who picks up everything and goes on a journey without knowing where he will wind up. The children of Israel go on a journey in the wilderness that not only brings them to the promised land but also forges their faith. Jesus's disciples go on a life-changing journey that starts with the simple words "Follow me." The journeys in the Bible are often geographic, but their primary purpose isn't just to move from one physical location to another. The primary purpose for the journey is personal, emotional, spiritual; the purpose is to take the person from where he or she is to where God intends him or her to be.

We are all on a journey. Maybe your personal journey is

vocational—you don't like what you do and you feel stuck, unable to imagine how much effort it would take to do something new. Maybe you are in a relationship journey—navigating through a divorce, a new marriage, or the death of someone you love. It is hard to imagine what life on the other side looks like. Maybe you are on an emotional journey. The trials you've endured, the tragedies you've suffered, and the transformations you've undergone are taking you somewhere new. They are making you *someone* new. That's a migration. Maybe some of you are dissatisfied with the life you have, or you believe that there has to be more. Maybe some of you have a vision for change; you can almost see what you want your life or your family or your company or your church to look like, but it is going to be a long haul to get there. These are all journeys, migrations from one place to another. And as with any journey, you will need a map, and it helps to have a guide. There is wisdom in listening to people who have traveled the same way.

The most famous migration story in scripture is the Exodus. It is the central story of the Hebrew scriptures. Jewish people still remember and share the story each year at Passover. Christians use the story as the basis for understanding Jesus. It has been depicted in movies for nearly every generation alive today. Why? Because the Exodus isn't just a story about Hebrew slaves migrating to a promised land. It isn't just a story about their journey. It is a story about our journey as well.

The Exodus starts where any good migration story has to start—with a person being convinced that it is time to leave home, that it is time to go. That all the excuses—all the reasons why now is not the right time—are lies. The migration starts when we step out and leave what is familiar, comfortable, and predictable. It starts with overcoming inertia and all that keeps us stuck. It starts with a burning bush, something so out of the ordinary that it forces us to finally move. It starts with one person: Moses.

MOSES AND THE BURNING BUSH

Before he was a great father of the faith and central figure in the Bible, he was just a guy with a family and a job and a predictable future. But before *that*, he had already lived an eventful life.

You probably know the story. After Pharaoh ordered the killing of all the male babies of the Hebrew slaves in Egypt, Moses's mother and sister placed him in a watertight basket and set him in a spot on the Nile where they knew Pharaoh's daughter regularly came to bathe. Just as they had hoped, Pharaoh's daughter found the helpless infant, felt compassion for him, and decided to rescue him even though she suspected that he was one of the Hebrew babies her father had ordered to be killed.

The Bible doesn't even tell us the name of Pharaoh's daughter. But thanks to her act, Moses grows up in Pharaoh's household. He has the lifestyle of a prince of Egypt. Unlike the slaves who harvest Pharaoh's crops and build Pharaoh's cities, Moses gets to eat the choicest food, wear the best clothes, and live in the palace with servants who wait on him.

Yet Moses also becomes aware that he is actually a

Hebrew. Once he knows that, it tears at him to see the way his fellow Israelites are treated. And one day, when he sees an Egyptian brutally beating a Hebrew, he snaps. He kills the Egyptian and buries his body in the sand. But there are witnesses. Pharaoh finds out and plans to have Moses executed.

We have moments when life beckons us to stop because something extraordinary has happened. And God can speak to us there.

So Moses embarks on what is actually the first of several huge journeys in his life. He runs away from Egypt. He ventures out alone into the Sinai Desert. And he winds up in a place called Midian. He starts a new life there and settles down. He gets married. He has a son. He goes to work for his father-in-law, who is a prominent man in the area. He has left all the turmoil of Egypt behind for good. He's in a comfortable routine, and he seems happy with his life. That is, until he finds out that God has other plans and places a call on his life, a call to pick up everything and embark on a new journey.

I remember clearly a day that changed everything for me. It was a day in late March during my senior year of college. I was preparing to graduate from Washington University in

St. Louis with a degree in mathematics. My emphasis was on theoretical math, to be precise. The time was coming when I had to turn this "theoretical" stuff into practice. I needed to find a job. I had several successful interviews in fields ranging from actuarial science and investment banking to code breaking with the National Security Agency. I just needed to decide which career path was best for me. As I look back now, I see it was an enviable situation. The economy was good, I had several great offers, and all I needed to do was choose. Jobs like these are what my math degree had been preparing me for, and now it was time to take the next step. This should have been easy. Except it wasn't.

I agonized over the decision. My parents had invested a lot of money in my education and rightfully wanted to know my plans for the future. I watched as my classmates and friends decided on graduate schools or job offers. I envied others who knew their next step with such confidence. Then there was me. I was about to have a degree, I had plenty of good opportunities, and yet I felt lost. I had no idea what I wanted to do. Perhaps even worse, I wasn't sure I wanted to do anything. I don't mean that I wanted to just sit around. But I wasn't sure I was ready to grow up, to get a "real job," and to settle in. But practical concerns were beginning to take over. It was too late to apply to the Peace Corps. I didn't have the money to backpack across Europe and reflect, and I was too proud to move back home to give myself some time to figure it all out. I needed to make a decision, and I couldn't. What I decided here would define the rest of my life—or so I thought. The trajectory of my future could be dictated by this one choice. My happiness was riding on not screwing this one up. I felt the pressure to choose well, and yet I was frozen by indecision.

Looking back on that time now, I recognize that there are far worse situations to be in. But for me that day, as the pressure mounted and I sensed the swirl of expectations all around me, it felt like the biggest crisis in the world. I suppose that, for me at age twenty-one, it was the one of the biggest crises I had ever faced in my life.

The weight of all of this was on my back that spring day as I walked to the bus stop to head to class. As I sat on the bus and watched buildings zoom by, the bus made a stop, as it always did, right in front of the St. Louis Cathedral. It's a huge, beautiful Romanesque-style Catholic church, and the Basilica was a building I had passed by hundreds of times before. This day was no different, except something happened. As I sat there staring at the church, I heard a voice, not quite audible, but very intelligible. The voice was trying to get my attention. I stared at the building and felt as if it were speaking to me and summoning me to stop what I was doing and to come inside. I promptly got off the bus at the next stop, backtracked, and made my way inside the church.

Once inside, I didn't know what to do. So I sat in silence and just listened. I don't remember how long I was there, maybe thirty minutes. I prayed, and I walked back outside. Nothing seemed to be different as I got back on the bus. But as we pulled away from the stop, I sensed that whatever I was to do next, it was going to have something to do with ministry. I sensed on that bus ride that God was telling me to go to seminary. I didn't know where that would lead or what I would end up doing. I didn't even really know what seminary entailed. But I had the sense that it was supposed to be my next step. Up until now, I had never really given this idea any consideration. That is why my parents had a blank look on their face when I told them the news. It is why my friends cocked their head with a puzzled look when I told them of my plans. It is why my fiancée (and now wife) asked me, "Are you sure?" It was because nothing that I had been preparing for had pointed to this. It felt like I was stepping away from everything that I knew I was prepared for and knew I was good at, and I was stepping out without a clear sense of where I was headed. It felt like the beginning of some completely different journey. But it started in the midst of crisis and with the sense that God was speaking to me there. For me, it was a burning-bush experience. Something as routine as passing by a building on the bus turned into something holy, where God got my attention and started me on a new journey.

Have you ever had a burning-bush moment? Have you ever had an experience in which you were going about the daily tasks of life, and then suddenly and rather unexpectedly God used the circumstances of your life to get your attention? That is what happened to Moses one day. Moses was going about his usual routine, tending his father-in-law's sheep, when God used something ordinary to nudge him to consider a journey that was completely unexpected. Here's how the Book of Exodus describes this event:

Now Moses was tending the flock of Jethro his father-in-law, the priest of Midian, and he led the flock to the far side of the wilderness and came to Horeb, the mountain of God. There the angel of the LORD appeared to him in flames of fire from within a bush. Moses saw that though the bush was on fire it did not burn up. So Moses thought, "I will go over and see this strange sight—why the bush does not burn up." When the LORD saw that he had gone over to look, God called to him from within the bush, "Moses! Moses!" And Moses said, "Here I am." (Exodus 3:1-4 NIV)

I believe that we all have burning-bush moments. Maybe they are messes of our making or circumstances beyond our control. Most often they are some combination of the two. We don't always recognize them for what they are, at least not right away. But we have moments when life beckons us to stop because something extraordinary has happened. And God can speak to us there.

SEVERAL EXCELLENT EXCUSES

I am a firm believer that God still speaks to people. Rarely will God speak through an audible noise (though I wouldn't rule that out). But it is a nudge, a growing internal sense of direction, a developing passion that needs to be followed, or a gnawing discontent that you have to do something about. God still speaks and calls us to leave behind the status quo in our lives and move in a new direction. But in the burning-bush moments of our lives, if we really listen, we can hear.

And who knows? Maybe Moses had a gnawing sense

all along that he shouldn't just leave his fellow Israelites to their fate. Maybe the sense of injustice that led him to kill the Egyptian had never really gone away. But maybe he had tried to put it all out of his mind, tried to stop listening, until God did something to demand his attention. Once Moses stopped to listen, he heard God speaking out of the bush.

> Then the LORD said, "I've clearly seen my people oppressed in Egypt. I've heard their cry of injustice because of their slave masters. I know about their pain. I've come down to rescue them from the Egyptians in order to take them out of that land and bring them to a good and broad land, a land that's full of milk and honey, a place where the Canaanites, the Hittites, the Amorites, the Perizzites, the Hivites, and the Jebusites all live. Now the Israelites' cries of injustice have reached me. I've seen just how much the Egyptians have oppressed them. So get going. I'm sending you to Pharaoh to bring my people, the Israelites, out of Egypt." (Exodus 3:7-10)

The assignment was clear. God wanted Moses to leave home, the place where he had gotten comfortable, started a family, worked, and made a life. God wanted him to leave that place behind and go let God use him to lead the Hebrew people out of slavery in Egypt into a new and more promising land. The assignment was ambitious, but it was clear.

People often lament to me that they wish God would speak to them clearly, the way God did to Moses. We often want to hear God as clearly and audibly as it seems Moses did. Why can't we have a burning bush, some unmistakable sign from God so we know what we're supposed to do? In the absence of that, we are left wondering whether the nudge is really from God. Is the "call" we are feeling really from God, or is it just our own? We can get paralyzed with this sort of analysis, and more often than not, it is a distraction. It is a stall tactic that keeps us from really having to do what we know we are supposed to do.

And more often than not, the clarity of the call is not our problem. We usually know what we need to do. We have a sense of the direction we need to take. We have clarity about what move we are being asked to consider. Our problem is courage. We know what to do or where to go, we just aren't sure we can do it (or that we even really want to try). So when we are scared, we begin the work of convincing ourselves why we can't do what we know we've been called to do, instead of why we can accomplish it. We come up with excuses about why now is not the right time or why the conditions aren't quite what we need them to be.

We aren't alone in that. It is exactly what Moses did. Upon hearing God call him to travel to Pharaoh and lead the people out of Egypt, Moses immediately begins coming up with excuses about why he can't. His excuses are worth reading because I think we use a lot of the same ones today.

Excuse 1

> *But Moses said to God, "Who am I to*
> *go to Pharaoh and to bring the Israelites*
> *out of Egypt?"*
> (Exodus 3:11)

11

This is the oldest objection in the book: "There is no way *I* could do something like *that*." When faced with an opportunity to do something risky or bold in our lives, nearly every one of us will first question our own capacity. This is exactly what is going on with Moses. After absorbing the gravity of what God is calling him to do, his first reaction is to call into question his own abilities. We all do this.

As we start imagining potential challenges, we also start creating reasons why we are likely not to be able to overcome those challenges. We defeat ourselves before we even try.

So many journeys in our life look crazy when they first come to us, whether it is a call to a certain job, the invitation to think about an opportunity, or the daydream we have about a new direction in our life. Almost immediately we start talking ourselves out of it; we start listing reasons why *we* can't do *that*. We run into a lot of fears over the course of our journey, but perhaps the first one is the fear of inadequacy. We get scared. The opportunity or call sounds exciting, but who are we to do it? We question everything from our ability to our capacity. Perhaps deep down we are afraid of looking silly, afraid of failing, or afraid of having to confront some of our own shortcomings. Whatever the reason, if you ever find yourself wondering if you can do something like that, then you know what Moses was up against.

Excuse 2

> *But Moses said to God, "If I now come to the Israelites and say to them, 'The God of your ancestors has sent me to you,' they are going to ask me, 'What's this God's name?' What am I supposed to say to them?"*
> (Exodus 3:13)

Now Moses turns his attention to what other people might think of this idea. If Moses actually says yes, he is going to have to tell his wife, his family, and his friends about his plan. Furthermore, when he gets to Egypt, he is going to have to convince the Hebrew elders and leaders of this whole burning-bush call. Ideas can seem fine in the private space of prayer but can suddenly sound crazy in the light of day. So Moses starts to consider the potential reactions people might have, and he comes up with his next objection. What is the essence of this excuse? I really think that, for Moses, he is already beginning to think about those who will doubt him. What is he supposed to do about the doubters?

I (unfortunately) think about doubters and people who will be skeptical of my plans more than I care to admit. I bet you do too. We are all concerned to some extent with what others will think of us. When it comes to a dramatic change in our life, it is natural to begin wondering what others will think. Some people will certainly question us or our sanity or both. And if they do question us, what are we going to say? In Moses's case, he imagines having to tell a group of Hebrew slaves that God has sent him to free them. They are almost certainly going to be skeptical; there are going to be doubters. They might even laugh in his face. The people are going to want to know who this "god" is who sent Moses. They are going to think he is crazy. Who wants to set themselves up for that?

The same thing will happen with us. As soon as we go public with a big change in our lives, inevitably there are going to be people around us who think we are nuts, especially if we bring faith into the decision. There are always doubters. Knowing how to deal with doubters, and what to say to them, can be intimidating, especially when we are questioning ourselves right alongside them.

Excuse 3

> *Then Moses replied, "But what if they don't believe me or pay attention to me? They might say to me, 'The LORD didn't appear to you!'"*
> (Exodus 4:1)

This objection really is an extension of the previous one. As soon as you admit that you sense God calling you to do something new in your life, people will wonder what voice you are really listening to. They'll want to know, "Who is this so-called god?" Is it the god of restlessness, the god of dissatisfaction, the god of running away, or the god of immediate gratification? Is this voice we are supposedly listening to really God, or is it merely our own? People who love us will ask this. It is a fair question.

Moses knows that he will hear these questions as soon as he shares this crazy-sounding idea. When he tells people that God told him to do it, they are going to wonder. They are going to have trouble believing it, and they may even accuse Moses of simply using God to do something that is self-serving. Moses is putting this question in the mouths of others, but I suspect that even Moses himself questioned whether he was really hearing from God. Was the idea to go to Egypt a divine voice? Or was this simply Moses giving voice to his own desire? Can Moses be sure that the voice he hears isn't coming from inside his own head, speaking to him from some kind of daydream about freeing his people from their plight?

That is a hard question. Like Moses, I often wonder if a decision I am about to make is from God or from my own heart. A few years ago, I led our congregation through a discernment process about our church facilities. After much prayer, discussion, and study, I believed that God was calling our church to build a new church facility. The project was ambitious, the cost was greater than anything we had ever done before, and the process was going to take years. Despite the challenges, I was convinced that this was the direction God wanted our church to take. But I was scared to share that with people. They almost certainly would question how I knew it was God's will. What if it was just my idea? What "god" was telling me to do this?

The same will be true for you after your own burning-bush

experience. When you do something big, immediately people are going to start questioning your idea and especially how you arrived at this decision. In these moments, we will question what voice we are really listening to and whether or not we really heard from God at all.

Excuse 4

> *But Moses said to the* LORD, *"My Lord, I've*
> *never been able to speak well, not yesterday,*
> *not the day before, and certainly not now since*
> *you've been talking to your servant. I have a slow*
> *mouth and a thick tongue."*
> (Exodus 4:10)

I call this a technical objection. Moses considers what God wants him to do and comes up with what he thinks is the ideal excuse. He doesn't speak well. Maybe he stutters. He's not going to be able to inspire the people with a stirring speech the way a great leader could. God wants him to go back and tell Pharaoh something. Perfect. Moses would love to do this, except for one little thing: he isn't good at talking. So instead of getting creative, offering to learn, or asking God for help, Moses just bows out. "I would love to help you out, God, but I have a thick tongue so it won't work. I guess you'll need to find somebody else."

It is almost comical to hear Moses's lack of creativity when it comes to answering God's call. As he mulls the idea over in his head, Moses wants to bail at the first sign of difficulty. It is as if speaking eloquently is the biggest challenge in this whole endeavor. Talking well is the least of Moses's concerns, but he fixates on that, and it becomes his reason not to respond. It would be funny if it weren't so true.

We do the same thing in our own lives. When we are called to make a change or head out in a new and uncertain direction, it is natural to begin anticipating what the challenges and obstacles might be. And to a certain degree it might be healthy to look ahead and think about the obstacles we might face. But that can also get us into trouble. As we start imagining potential challenges, we also start creating reasons why we are likely not to be able to overcome those challenges. Pretty soon, if we aren't careful, we can come up with imaginary reasons why we can't overcome imaginary problems. We defeat ourselves before we even try.

Excuse 5

But Moses said, "Please, my Lord, just send someone else."
(Exodus 4:13)

This one really isn't even an excuse as much as it is an outright objection—or maybe a confession. "God, can't you just find someone else to do this? I really can't and don't want to."

In my line of work, I have a lot of occasions to ask people to consider doing things that are outside their comfort zone. Maybe it is speaking in public, praying with others, or playing music in front of an entire congregation. Like Moses, they will often rehearse their reasons and excuses about why they can't accommodate the request. On a good day, I will address and answer every one of these objections. And they often will say something like this: "Well, I'll tell you what, if you can't find anyone else to do it, then maybe I will consider it."

Have you ever said that? I know that I have. It is a more polite form of Moses's plea. "God, can't you find someone else?" And certainly God could have found someone. God could have asked anyone. But the fact remains that God asked Moses to do it. This isn't a call for other people. It is a call for Moses, and Moses will have to reckon with it.

> *When we're called to embark on some journey in life, we need to remember to factor God into our calculations.*

Similarly, we can get distracted when considering change in our life. And sometimes we just wish that someone else could do it. Often, a call in our life starts out as a dissatisfaction with the way things are—and the belief that maybe we could do something about it.

In 2015 Michael Brown Jr. was shot by a police officer in the St. Louis suburb of Ferguson. The news went global, and suddenly white people were faced with questions that they preferred to ignore. Suddenly, many people were waking up to the ways that racism has infected everything from municipal court practices to police profiling. Many people in my church and all around St. Louis began asking how they could respond.

I listened to a lot of bold ideas, courageous ways in which people felt called to make a difference. But as is often the case with big, overwhelming, systemic issues, it is easy for initial enthusiasm to wane. I would often hear people assume that somewhere, out there, in a city full of millions, someone else was certainly on top of this. That person was likely better qualified, had more expertise, had the time, and was better positioned to bring the idea to fruition. Without expressing it quite like Moses did, we often assume that, if we come up with an important idea, certainly God has someone else better qualified who can do the job.

As I read Moses's excuses, I am reminded of how easy it is for me to do the same when confronted with a journey that seems overwhelming and daunting. I share a lot of the same excuses that Moses offered to God (and several that he didn't). So what are your excuses? As you consider a big change in your life and feel the fear welling up inside you, what are the objections you have raised to yourself? I bet some of you are telling yourself the timing is just not right. You would do it, and you want to do it, and one day you *will* do it, but now isn't the right time. Maybe you need to get through school, get the wedding over with, wait until the kids go off to college, or hold off until you have more financial security. Maybe it is a busy season for you, or you have too much on your plate already. Maybe you need to be there for your parents, kids, or friends. Maybe you'll do it as soon as this project is over or tax season is through. The list goes on. I understand that.

For some of us, maybe what holds us back are concerns about resources. We don't have the money, or the sacrifice would be too costly for us. For some of us, the issue is comfort. We fear giving up the known for the unknown. For some of us, it may be the security of the status quo that keeps us from responding.

But behind all of Moses's objections was really one fear—the fear of inadequacy. Ultimately, Moses was afraid that he would fail. He was afraid that he didn't have the skills, knowledge, leadership, or capability to do what God was calling him to do. (And who among us would not have felt the same way? God wasn't just asking Moses to take on a new role in his life. He was asking him to go back to a place he had left years ago fearing for his life. He was asking him to go the court of Pharaoh, the most powerful ruler on earth, and tell him to release thousands of Israelites from slavery.)

Moses was afraid that, if people questioned him, he wouldn't have answers they could believe. He was scared that his effort would be met with challenges that he couldn't overcome. He was scared that he didn't have the gifts and skills that he would need to complete the task. He was scared that, although he wanted to do something significant, he wasn't actually the best person for the mission. Certainly someone, somewhere, would be better than him. All of this is the fear of inadequacy. It is a fear of not having what it takes. It is a fear of failing. But it is more than failing at a task. It is the fear of finding out that we failed as people, that we couldn't do it. And that fear keeps so many of us from stepping out in the first place. We would rather maintain the illusion that we could have done it but simply chose not to. We're so afraid of falling short that we don't even try.

While Moses was so busy coming up with reasons why he couldn't do it, he was ignoring all the reasons why he was actually the perfect candidate for the job. Moses was made for this. In fact, if anyone was ideal for the job of going to Pharaoh, it was Moses. He knew Pharaoh personally. He knew how Pharaoh thought. Because he had grown up in the royal palace, he knew the ways of the court and how the bureaucracy worked. And as an Israelite, he knew about the sufferings of his people. When God called on him, all that Moses could think about were reasons why he was the wrong choice. But in the midst of Moses's excuses, God saw a different reality. There's a lesson in that for us, too. Our own doubts and anxieties may cause us to miss the different reality that God recognizes but we can't yet see. Maybe there's a reason God called us into something new. Maybe we actually were made for this.

If you are contemplating something new and bold in your life, the fear of inadequacy will hit you just as it hit Moses. Your objections may be unique to your situation, but the underlying fear is one that we all face. Facing this fear is where we begin, because unless we overcome it, we will never even get to experience what the journey is really like. And don't forget: while you might be spending all this time and energy thinking up excuses why you can't do it, you may be ignoring all the reasons why you are actually perfect for this journey!

So how did God respond to Moses? What did God say that ultimately led Moses, even with all of his objections, to say yes and go back to Egypt? What was it that led Moses to step away from home and job, family and friends, safety and security, and head out to a place that would stir up every fear? The answer is surprisingly simple. While God responded to each one of Moses's objections in a specific way, there was really only one response. Just as there was one underlying fear with Moses, there was one overarching response from God: "I will be with you."

Think about it. When Moses first objected to God, what did God say?

> But Moses said to God, "Who am I to go to Pharaoh and bring the Israelites out of Egypt?" God said, "I'll be with you." (Exodus 3:11-12a)

When Moses wondered about God's name, or asked about doubters, or confessed his inability to speak, in each instance God's promise was the same. I will be there with you. *I* will give you *my* name, *I* will perform signs through you, *I* will give you the power to do things you couldn't otherwise do, and *I* will lift up others to help you. In other words, God said to Moses: "You are scared of not being enough, of being inadequate, of not having the skills or not being able to overcome the challenges. But here's the thing: you aren't doing this alone." That is the whole point of Moses's call story. Moses is weighing all the options *as if* he has to do this whole thing alone. But God is making it clear that he *doesn't* have to do it alone. What Moses is forgetting to factor into his calculations is the power of God. Moses doesn't have the power to convince the Israelites to listen, but God does. Moses doesn't have the power to make an impression on Pharaoh, but God does.

When we're called to embark on some journey in life, we need to remember to factor God into our calculations too. Here's the thing. God doesn't call us to do things that we can accomplish on our own. God doesn't call us to surmount obstacles, accept challenges, go through transitions, make changes, or set out on journeys that we have the capacity to manage all on our own. What would be the point? No. God always calls us to do things that we *cannot* do on our own. Why? Because these journeys require God, will teach us to rely on God, and will remind us that God is with us. These journeys, like the one Moses is being called to begin, are impossible if we embark on them alone. That is why we are scared. That is why we feel inadequate. That is why we are nervous and stalling. But we've forgotten. We aren't doing this alone. And that knowledge changes everything.

It shouldn't be lost on us that, when God sent Jesus into the world to save us, the name given to him in the Gospel of Matthew was Emmanuel, which means "God with us." And it isn't a mistake that at the very end of that same gospel, the last words that Jesus spoke were these: "And remember, I am with you always, to the end of the age" (Matthew 28:20 NRSV).

Nearly every person in the Bible who began a significant

journey had the same basic fear—that they weren't enough. And every time God's promise has remained the same, "I am with you." Nearly forty years after Moses would lead the people through the desert, the next generations of Israelites were scared to cross the river Jordan and enter into the promised land. Their leader, Moses's protégé, Joshua, confessed this fear to God. God's words back to Joshua have inspired generations of people over thousands of years to endure, overcome, or accomplish the impossible. We will close this chapter, and begin our journey, with the same words. Read them as if they were written to you and for you, because they were. "Have I not commanded you? Be strong and courageous. Do not be afraid; do not be discouraged, for the LORD your God will be with you wherever you go" (Joshua 1:9 NIV).

Chapter 2

THE LETTING GO

———⌇∿∿⌇———

*A journey of a thousand miles begins with a
single step.*
—Chinese Proverb

Parting is such sweet sorrow.
—William Shakespeare,
Romeo and Juliet

It goes without saying that, in order to change, grow,
move, or begin a new journey of any kind, you first
have to leave. You have to be willing to step away from
something if you are ever to experience anything new. Once
we muster up the will and courage to believe that we can
step out, that we can follow that nudge from God in our
life, then immediately we are faced with the challenge of
leaving. And many journeys are stopped right here, before
they ever begin. It never occurs to many of us that, before
we get *there*, we have to leave *here*. We can't have both. We
can't keep both. We can't have one foot here and one foot
there. A journey has to begin with a departure. Sometimes,
that first step is the hardest one of all. And as Shakespeare
wrote, leaving always includes some amount of sorrow, even
if it is for the promise of something better.

Think of how many biblical calls began with the

challenge of leaving. It's the call that Jesus issued to his disciples (and to others he invited to accompany him along the way): "Leave behind what you're doing, and come follow me." Perhaps the most famous example is the story of Abram, who was called some four hundred years before Moses was ever alive. It was such a life-changing experience that it even involved a change in names for Abram and his wife, Sarai, who became Abraham and Sarah when their journey with God began.

Here was the setting. Abram was seventy-five years old, married to his wife, Sarai, and living in the town of Haran, where his father had taken him. The Bible doesn't tell us much about Abram's early life, but we know that he had always wanted children. That dream hadn't become a reality for Abram and Sarai. Now he was seventy-five years old and settled into his life. Haran was home, and Abram had no reason to think he wouldn't spend the rest of his life right there, just like his father had done.

Suddenly one day Abram had his burning-bush moment. He was going about his day in Haran. No doubt it was a completely ordinary day. Then God showed up and called Abram to something crazy. It is recorded in Genesis 12:

> The LORD said to Abram, "Leave your land, your family, and your father's household for the land that I will show you. I will make of you a great nation and will bless you. I will make your name respected, and you will be a blessing. I will bless those who bless you, those who curse you I will curse; all the families of the earth will be blessed because of you." (Genesis 12:1-3)

I try to put myself in Abram's shoes, and it is really hard to imagine taking God seriously here. Abram was seventy-five years old! He had no children, despite decades of trying. He was growing old and ready to settle down. He had lived his life, and though he may have had years left (his father, Terah, lived to a ripe old age of 205), he had a pretty good idea what the latter part of his life would look like. And then God showed up making a crazy promise. God told Abram that he wanted to take him from his home and set him up in his own land. Not only that, but God was going to make a whole new nation of him and his family. God would bless Abram and Sarai with kids. In fact, a little later God took Abram outside and told him to look up. Just as you can't count all the stars in the sky, so Abram would not be able to count his offspring, God promised. It was an outlandish and audacious promise. It sounds crazy. Even though they had no children, and Sarai was past the usual age of childbearing, God was going to give this couple so many descendants that they would outnumber the stars in the sky. Wait—what? I mean Abram was faithful, but this was nuts. Why would he believe in something crazy like that?

It was not unlike the audaciousness of Moses's own burning-bush moment. It was outlandish to think that Moses, a fugitive turned shepherd, with a family and kids, was going to become a great liberator of an entire people and single-handedly defeat Pharaoh (who, by the way, had the most powerful army on earth at his disposal). But all of that lay far in the future for Moses, just as it took years for the promise of a child to come true for Abram and Sarai.

And just like the old Chinese proverb says, with Moses and Abram the greatest journey of their lives would begin with a single step: leaving home.

God is going to ask us to trust him first. Trust God without knowing where that will lead.

Someone asked me recently to explain the difference between a house and a home. I suspect you have thought about that. A house is just that, a physical structure. It has walls, a foundation, rooms, and doors. But it is inanimate. A house elicits little emotion. The word itself evokes nothing personal or warm. But a home is something entirely different. An ideal home is a place of love, a place of safety, a place of relationships and familiarity. Home is a place you can return to, a place you know inside and out. Home is dependable and secure. It is your comfort zone. Home is a place where you know the names of people, the places to go, and perhaps the places to avoid. Home is the spot that, though it might not be perfect (and it never is), is at least reliable. You know what to expect at home, and there is safety in knowing what to expect. There is a reason the word sparks emotion and connection. Home is a lot more than a place or a structure. Home is a set of conditions that in many ways we long for. We want to be home.

And yet what was God's first challenge to Abram? What

was God's first challenge to Moses? The first challenge—the one that would have to be met before the adventure could even begin—was to leave home.

THE FIRST STEP IS A BIG ONE

Sitting on that bus years ago as it rolled by the church, my burning-bush moment, I strongly sensed that God was calling me to forget everything I thought I would do with my life. Instead, God was calling me to pursue what was, at that time, a relatively late development: my interest in ministry. I knew that seminaries existed, but I didn't know much about them. What I did know is this: they were a far cry from the mathematics I had spent four years studying as the focus of my degree.

So I decided to quickly put together a spring trip to go visit a few seminaries. I figured that, if God was nudging me, I should at least go and see what a seminary is like. After all, up until this point, I had barely heard of them and never even been to one! My dad, my girlfriend (now wife), and I all set out on the trip. I remember touring one school; I think it was Yale Divinity. A student was showing us around on a tour, talking about the coursework, the classes, the student activities. When he was finished, I asked a pretty straightforward question:

"Is it hard?"

"Well, it is intense," the student replied, "but you can do it. It is just a lot of reading and writing and of course speaking—all things that I am sure you had to do a lot of in college."

And that is when my fear set in—because I had studied theoretical math! That is what I was good at. That is what I knew inside and out. That is what I knew I could succeed in and what I had spent four years (and a lot of money) preparing to do with the remainder of my life. And I don't mean to stereotype, but a lot of us math people study precisely because we aren't good at the reading, the writing, and especially the speaking. These are exactly the things that you don't do much of when you study math.

If that's the stereotype, it certainly fit me. I had grown up being exceptionally proficient in math—and less so in all the other disciplines. So what I had been told all my life is that I should pursue math because it's what I was good at. Although never said, what I absorbed from all this encouragement to pursue a future in math is that there was an array of disciplines that I wasn't so good at and that perhaps I shouldn't pursue careers that rely heavily on those. Whether adults around me meant that or not, I figured that I was wired to do something with numbers.

All that suddenly flooded my mind at the end of the tour at Yale. I thought to myself: *What in the world am I doing? I am stepping away from everything that I know I am good at. And I am about to step in to something that emphasizes, actually requires, excellence in all the things that I never felt particularly strong in. I am stepping out of my sweet spot and into, well, come to think of it, I don't even know what I am stepping into.*

And that was it. I didn't know where this call was taking me, but I knew that it was asking me to drop everything and follow. It was asking me to leave home, and I don't mean geographically. This nudge was asking me to leave behind what I knew, what was comfortable, known, predictable, safe, and familiar. And do you know what was most frightening? God was asking me to leave all of that without any guarantee of where exactly we were headed together.

That is what Abram was facing. Consider the very first thing God told him: "Leave your land, your family, and your father's household for the land that I will show you."

Leave your land—the place that is known, comfortable, and familiar and the place where you have friends, family, and connections. Leave all of that. And for what? For a land that I will show you. God wants Abram to leave a sure thing, and God won't even tell him where he is going! I am not sure how you operate, but typically I don't like to step away from something known and good and exchange that for something unknown. If I leave something behind, I would like to know what exactly it is that I am leaving for. But that is not the way God works. That is not the way faith works. Instead, God is going to ask us to trust him first. Trust God without knowing where that will lead.

BACK TO MOSES

So let's come back to Moses's story and the story of the Israelites. In the previous chapter, I introduced you to Moses and his call. We can all identify with his resistance to God's nudge. All of us have that inner voice that seems to prompt us to move forward, step out, and take risks. In the church, we believe it is more than an "inner voice." We believe those prompts come from God through the power of the Holy Spirit that resides inside each one of us. That nudge, as I like to call it, can sometimes be as direct, audible, and clear as the command given to Moses or Abram. More often than not, it is a slowly developing sense of purpose and awareness that finally builds to a crescendo—a moment when we have to make a decision to go for it or not.

If you have a particular change you feel called to make, then let's use that throughout this book. And if you don't, well, at some point you will. And maybe reading this book will help you realize that there is something brewing within you. Many of us are in the middle of significant transitions and need to know that what we feel and experience is not new. There are examples for how to weather those transitions and hope to be found in the witness of those who have gone before us.

The story of Moses and the Israelites in many ways forms the backbone of the Old Testament of the Bible. There are a lot of stories in the scriptures. But this is *the* story. Broadly speaking, the exodus story—that is, the journey of the Israelites from slavery in Egypt, into the wilderness and into the promised land, all under the leadership of Moses (and later a man named Joshua)—is a story that all other stories in the Bible in some way prefigure or echo. Even in the New Testament, Jesus uses the story of the exodus to interpret his own death and resurrection. Matthew's Gospel presents Jesus as a new Moses—one who, this time, delivers the people from bondage to sin and into a different kind of promised land.

So it makes sense that, as we learn about the exodus story and Moses's own journey with the Israelites, it will illuminate our own journeys. What Moses and the Israelites experienced, struggled with, and overcame is a direct analogy to our own spiritual journeys with God, and the changes that God calls us to make in our life. Abram's journey is a foreshadowing of the change and migration that God requires for all of God's people. God wants to take all of us to a "land that I will show you." But to do that, God asks all of us to leave behind "home," whatever that home looks like and feels like. It would be the story of Abram's (Abraham's) son Isaac and his grandson Jacob. It was true for Moses and the Israelites. It would be the story of Peter, Paul, and the rest of the disciples. And it will be no different for us.

Wishing for change never really changes anything. Change only occurs when you actually change!

When Moses left Midian, he was leaving behind the home he had made for himself there. After striking down an Egyptian guard and fleeing out of fear for his life, as you may remember from the previous chapter, Moses found a place to settle down in the land of Midian. There, he not only married but also was adopted into his wife's family. He had children, became a shepherd, and put down roots. Egypt, the place of Moses's birth, was now a scary and dangerous place for him. Midian was now his home, in every sense of the word.

But God was not content to leave Moses at home. With the call he received at the burning bush, Moses knew that the first step in following that call would be to leave the place that had become home for him. Exodus tells us that, immediately after hearing from God:

> Moses went back to his father-in-law Jethro and said to him, "Please let me go back to my family in Egypt and see whether or not they are still living." Jethro said to Moses, "Go in peace." The LORD said to Moses in Midian, "Go back to Egypt because everyone there who wanted to kill you has died." So Moses took his wife and his children, put them on a donkey, and went back to the land of Egypt. Moses also carried the shepherd's rod from God in his hand. (Exodus 4:18-20)

The first step in living into the new call—the first step to following the voice of God and responding to the nudge (or in Moses's case, the shove!)—was to leave.

But Moses's radical departure really was just a foreshadowing of what the Hebrew slaves were all going to have to do. Now is a good time to fill some of you in on the Hebrew people (who would later be formed into the kingdom of Israel). The Hebrews had migrated to Egypt some four hundred years prior to Moses, under the invitation of their fellow Israelite Joseph, who had become Pharaoh's right-hand man (that story made famous by Broadway's *Joseph and the Amazing Technicolor Dreamcoat*). Scared of their growing numbers and influence, the Egyptians enslaved the Hebrews after Joseph died. For several centuries they had been subject to oppression, forced labor, and mistreatment at the hands of the pharaohs. And over those centuries they had consistently prayed to God for release. That day was finally coming. God had called Moses to go back to Egypt and lead the Hebrew people in to a new promised land, a land "flowing with milk and honey."

When Moses arrived in Egypt, he went straight to Pharaoh to demand the release of the Hebrews. Not surprisingly, Pharaoh did not appreciate the demand. Rather than release the people, he made their lives even harder. He increased the brick-making quota and took away the straw that helped bind the bricks together. In other words, he made their work more difficult while taking away the tools they needed for the job. As you might imagine, the Hebrew people were not pleased with Moses's "leadership." While Moses was trying to lead them to freedom in a land that was all their own, they began to wonder if it was better just to stay put. Maybe, they thought, all that Moses had really done was to stir up trouble for them. The Israelite leaders finally brought their concerns to Moses in what would become their first in a long line of complaints:

> The Israelite supervisors saw how impossible their situation was when they were commanded, "Don't reduce your daily quota of bricks." When they left Pharaoh, they met Moses and Aaron, who were waiting for them. The supervisors said to them, "Let the LORD see and judge what you've done! You've made us stink

in the opinion of Pharaoh and his servants. You've given them a reason to kill us." Then Moses turned to the LORD and said, "My Lord, why have you abused this people? Why did you send me for this? Ever since I first came to Pharaoh to speak in your name, he has abused this people. And you've done absolutely nothing to rescue your people." (Exodus 5:19-23)

A theme emerges here that would come back to haunt Moses for nearly the rest of his life. The Israelites knew that Moses wanted to help them. They understood that he wanted to lead them somewhere new. They even seemed to believe that God had appointed Moses to take them to a land of freedom, a land all their own, full of good things. Furthermore, *they* had been praying for this! Freedom, release, their own land, and the ability to worship God freely: all of this they had been collectively praying for. Not for a few months, or even for decades, but they had been praying for it for four hundred years! Now, after all of that time, God finally heard their cries and was going to answer their prayer. God finally was going to lead them to something new. So God sent Moses, and Moses began the process of leading them away from slavery and toward a new life, in a new land. The people embraced Moses, they were ready, and they wanted this. And then, at the first sign of challenge, at the first obstacle they encountered, and at the first clue that this transition was not going to be easy, what did they do? They got scared. And in their fear, they began to complain to Moses. Their complaining revealed what was going through their heads: "Maybe the change is not worth it. Maybe the change is too hard. Maybe our current situation is not so bad after all. Maybe we should just stay here. After all, we at least know what to expect here. We at least know what things will be like. If we listen, if we follow, who knows what will happen. Who knows how long it will take? Who knows what it will cost us? Who knows where we will end up? Maybe it won't be worth it. Maybe we will end up worse off. No, let's just play it safe. Let's stay. Better the devil you know than the devil you don't."

And so for the first time (but not the last), they began to complain to Moses. Maybe this whole "going somewhere new" thing was overrated. This was a lot harder than any of them thought. And suddenly they began to think that staying put was preferable to the uncertainty of change. *After four hundred years of praying for something*, with that thing finally within reach, they essentially said "never mind" to God. We will just stay put.

WHY LEAVING HOME IS HARD

Does any of this sound familiar to you? It should. We display this attitude all the time. So many of us like to complain about our current life. We complain about our work, our friends, our spouse, our city, our financial situation, or our season of life. And it is easy to imagine something new. It is easy to peer over the fence at a new reality and say, "I wish I had that." It is easy to pray for something new. It is easy to hope that things change. Unfortunately, *actually* changing isn't easy at all. It is costly, it's hard, it's uncertain, and it's scary. But wishing for change never really changes anything. Change only occurs when, well, when you actually change!

Here is the first reason why change is hard (and, therefore, the first reason that moving into something new is hard): it requires you to leave home. As with Abram, Moses, and the Israelites, before you can move toward something new, you have to let go of home. And no matter what home is like, it is hard to leave.

It took me a while to understand this principle. I loved the house that I grew up in. I have great parents who were always supportive of me. I had great friends in high school, and the small town in which I was raised never really felt constricting. I loved it all. That is my image of home. So leaving home for me was hard because home meant comfort, support, community, warmth, and security. This is a lot like Abram. We have no reason to believe he didn't love his home. Moses was secure and comfortable, too, after he settled in Midian. He didn't want to leave. But for God to do something new with him and through him, he was asked first to leave it behind.

But I also know people who didn't have a good home life growing up. Some of you can relate. Maybe home conjures up memories of dysfunctional relationships, fighting, or financial insecurity. Many people grow up feeling alone, isolated, or bullied by friends. Some of us may have grown up around violence, unpredictability, and fear. In those cases, home is not a place we think of warmly. That is more like what the Israelites experienced. In fact, home for them meant violence, slavery, chains, and even death. That makes it all the more incredible that, even with such a negative reality all around them, *it was still hard for them to leave*!

Why? Because even if home is not supportive, loving, or warm, it is still a known quantity. Home is still predictable. At least with home, the fear of the unknown is at bay. And this leads to one of the many counterintuitive principles around change and moving into a new reality. Even if your current situation sucks, you will still have fears when it comes to leaving it behind. Even if you know your current situation is not what you want or isn't good for you or is holding you back, it is still hard to leave it. It is hard to leave for the same reason that it was hard for the Israelite slaves to leave. Your current situation is at least familiar. And the alternative, the new thing, could land you in an even worse spot. And so either way, whether home means something positive or something negative, home is still what you know. And it is hard for us to leave what is known and familiar. But leaving the home is exactly what God called Abram, Moses, and the Israelite slaves to do. And leaving the comfort of "home" is exactly what God is calling you to do.

YOUR HOME

I remember years ago sitting down with a couple who were struggling in their relationship. They had been dating each other for years. She was invested in his family, and he was invested in hers. They had bought a house together, planned a life together, and were now considering getting married. There was just one problem. The relationship wasn't working. They fought, a lot. They had very different visions for marriage and kids. They seemed to value life in very different ways. In addition to all of this, I noticed that the way they talked to each other would be considered by many to be verbally abusive. It was one of the few times that I have ever directly challenged a couple. I said to them, "It seems to me that, as much as you want to be together and to get married, you don't actually like each other. You speak to each other in pretty awful ways, and your fights don't seem to be productive or get you anywhere new in your relationship. Why do you want to get married?"

There was silence. Then they started to answer the question. They talked about how much they had invested in their relationships. The woman started backpedaling on the negative talk and reminded me that, most of the time, things between them were actually good. The guy thought that any relationship would look like this, with its ups and downs. So I decided to do something. I met with each of them separately and asked them the same questions. When they were apart, their answers changed. For the woman, she was watching her friends get married, and a few of them were having kids. She wanted that as well. She was afraid that, if she ended this relationship, she wouldn't find anyone else, or at least not in the time frame that she had mapped out in her head. For the guy, as hard as the relationship was, it provided companionship. He was afraid of being alone. He didn't say it that way, but in every answer he gave there was a fear of having to wade through life being single and alone. He was a guy who was always with someone.

In the end it became clear to me that even though their

relationship wasn't great, and in an ideal world they would likely desire a different relationship, they were nonetheless scared to end it. They were scared to leave what they had invested in, what was predictable, comfortable, and known. The truth is, the unknown nature of what breaking up would mean for each of them was enough to keep them staying put, even in a situation that they knew wasn't good for either of them. For this couple, "home" was a relationship that provided some sense of normalcy and predictability. They wanted something better and, inside, each of them knew that God was calling them to something different and new. But leaving home was overwhelming and scary.

I could see it. I gently and compassionately named it for them. Fortunately, they eventually saw it as well. They decided not to get married. Years later, I had the honor of actually presiding over a wedding for the woman and her eventual husband. She met a guy who was right for her. And even though it wasn't on her time line, it was better and more fulfilling than anything she had experienced in her prior relationship. But that doesn't mean that it wasn't hard getting there. After all when she left the former relationship, she didn't know what the future would hold. She didn't know if there would be something better out there. She didn't know if the pain and emotional turmoil would be worth it. At the time, the future looked uncertain, and home seemed certain. In those moments, it is all too easy to do what the Israelites wanted to do—to just stay put, even in the midst of circumstances that aren't good for you. But leaving home was worth it for them. And it will be worth it for you.

I want you to consider the change you are feeling called to make or the call you are feeling nudged to follow. I promise you that somewhere in that call will be an invitation to leave something familiar, predictable, and known. That is your "home." Maybe home is a relationship that you know is not healthy and right, and yet leaving it could mean loneliness— an even scarier proposition. Maybe home for you is a job that is unfulfilling, uninspiring, and burning you out. But to leave it is scary because at least it is a predictable workload and dependable paycheck. Maybe home for you is sticking to a set of activities that you know you can do and are good at. The thought of following a call might mean giving up your sweet spot to try something that you may not be great at. Maybe home for you is only taking on challenges you know you can accomplish. Trying anything bigger, better, or new could mean failure.

What is the home that you cling closely to? And what would it mean for you to leave that behind? What would it mean for you, like Abram, to trust that, as you step away from what is known and predictable, God will indeed lead you somewhere new and better? As you begin that journey, challenges will inevitable come. Usually, they will come right out of the gate.

For me, leaving home for the sake of a call first felt like stepping away from what I knew I was good at and instead taking a step toward something unknown, something I wasn't sure I could do, and something that could very well mean struggle or even failure. Since that time, I have had countless moments when God was calling me to take a next step. But the step toward one thing meant a step away from something else. It will be like that with God.

And here is the thing that I imagine is most scary. Rarely does God show us what the future will be like *before* we leave something else behind. That is, usually we don't leave home with a clear vision of what is coming next. God wants us, like Abram, to leave home now for a land that he will show us. That means that we first have to step out, with no certainty of what the ground ahead will look like. That is the true definition of trust and faith. And it is that stepping out, without knowing where you will land, that we turn to next.

Chapter 3

THE LEAP OF FAITH

There is a great scene near the end of the movie *Indiana Jones and the Last Crusade* that I think is worth remembering whenever God calls us on a journey. In the scene, Jones is racing to help his injured father. He is navigating his way through a cave when he suddenly reaches a deep chasm. Above him is a lion's head carved into stone. Jones consults his guidebook, which offers this vague clue: "Only in the leap from the lion's head will he prove his worth."

Jones is stumped. He can't leap from the lion's head. The gap is much too wide, and he would never be able to jump across it (or swing over it with the aid of his famous whip). He mutters to himself that it is impossible to make this leap. He can't understand what options are left for him. Suddenly he hears his friends yelling. There is not much time left. If he is to help his father, he cannot stay where he is. He has to try to cross the divide. Finally, he says to himself, "It's a leap of faith."

With his hurt father praying, "You must believe," Jones dramatically raises his foot off of the cave floor and takes one giant step into the air. As he is lowering his foot with all its force, and when you believe he is going to plunge directly down the chasm to what would certainly be his death, his foot suddenly lands on a solid stone surface. The stone pathway isn't visible at first, but it is there. It provides a safe place for his foot to land. Once he has stepped out in faith, he is able to cross this seemingly unbridgeable gap.

In the previous chapter I described the story of Abram and his challenge from God to leave home. Part of what made that a challenge is what we've already talked about, which is abandoning something comfortable, known, and predictable. But what makes this call doubly difficult is that God wouldn't tell Abram what he was leaving *for*. Remember? God says, "Leave your land, your family, and your father's household for the land that I will show you" (Genesis 12:1).

For the land that I will show you? What? If I were Abram, I would have had a follow-up question: "Uh, God, what is this 'land you will show me'? Can you just show it to me now, before I go to all this effort to pack up and leave home? I would like to see what I am getting myself into."

But that is not what God does. Instead, God expects Abram to pull an Indiana Jones. To step *first* and to find out where he will land later. It is a true leap of faith. It isn't the first time, and it certainly is not the last time that God will require someone to step out first, before knowing exactly where one's foot will land. God did it with Abram, he did it with Moses and the Israelites, and he will do it with you.

THE LEGEND OF NAHSHON

Nahshon is not exactly a household name, even for those of you who have read the Bible before. He is mentioned only a few times in all of scripture, and we have scant details about who he was or what he did. We do know, however, that Nahshon was one of Moses's key leaders. Before I share more about Nahshon, let's quickly recap what happened with Moses and the Israelites. When we visited them last, Moses had returned to Egypt and confronted Pharaoh. The results weren't great. Pharaoh punished the people with harder labor, and the people complained to Moses. They wanted to stay put in Egypt, even though Egypt meant slavery, rather than risk the unknown of standing up to Pharaoh and stepping out in faith. But that didn't last long. They decided to stick with Moses, with the promise that God would lead them out of slavery and into a promised land.

Pharaoh wasn't real keen on letting them go.

But God showed up through Moses, just as God had promised. God brought plagues (ten of them in all) until Pharaoh finally relented and allowed the Hebrew slaves to leave—that is, before he changed his mind (or "hardened his heart") one final time and decided to send his army to bring the Israelites back. Now the Bible tells us that there were more than six hundred thousand male Israelites who left Egypt with Moses (Numbers 1:46). That is a lot of people to lead on a cross-country walking journey to a new land. This was not going to be a secret escape. In fact, if you add women and children, the number of people "escaping" Egypt likely amounted to well over a million. Moses was going to need some help!

Which brings us to Nahshon. The people of Israel were

divided into tribes, and each tribe had a chief or leader. The Book of Numbers tells us that Nahshon was the leader of the tribe of Judah. From the Bible we learn a little bit about his relatives, but the scriptures tell us nothing else about Nahshon himself.

But there is a legend about Nahshon that isn't in the Bible. Instead, it is part of the Jewish Midrash (that is, the commentaries by early rabbis on the Hebrew scriptures that we call the Old Testament). The legend involves the moment when the Israelites were escaping and came to the shore of the Red Sea. As the people neared the shore, they realized that Pharaoh's army was pursuing them. The army's chariots were gaining on the long, slow train of Israelites. The people could see the dust stirred up by the chariots and horses; they could gauge how the army was closing the distance between them. They faced the impassible sea on one side and a powerful army on the other. Without time to find or build boats, it looked as if there was no way forward for the Israelites. They were trapped. And, naturally, they were afraid. The Bible story tells us what they did:

> As Pharaoh drew closer, the Israelites looked back and saw the Egyptians marching toward them. The Israelites were terrified and cried out to the LORD. They said to Moses, "Weren't there enough graves in Egypt that you took us away to die in the desert? What have you done to us by bringing us out of Egypt like this? Didn't we tell you the same thing in Egypt? 'Leave us alone! Let us work for the Egyptians!' It would have

been better for us to work for the Egyptians than to die in the desert." (Exodus 14:10-12)

If this feels like déjà vu, that's because this is the same complaint we just heard in the previous chapter. But there's one important difference this time. When Moses came back to Egypt and announced that God was going to deliver them from slavery, the people had plenty of reason to be skeptical at first. But then they saw God's power revealed through the plagues that God brought upon Egypt. When they actually began to leave, they weren't being asked to take a totally blind leap of faith. They were being asked to trust in a God who had already demonstrated the power to rescue them. And yet, as soon as they saw Pharaoh's army coming, they forgot about all of that. They forgot everything they'd had a chance to learn about God. Instead, they got scared. Their fear turned to panic. After all they'd already seen and been through, they were ready to go back to the slavery they had always known. It's a pattern that repeats itself over and over in this story. Fear often causes us to forget where we've been, what God has already brought us through, and the challenges we've already been able to overcome. Each time trouble, a challenge, or an obstacle comes their way, the people question their choice to have ever left in the first place.

But Moses encouraged them, asking them to trust God (even though he wasn't exactly sure how God was going to get them out of this one). Moses brought his concern to God, and, finally, God intervened: "Then the LORD said to Moses, 'Why do you cry out to me? Tell the Israelites to get moving.

As for you, lift your shepherd's rod, stretch out your hand over the sea, and split it in two so that the Israelites can go into the sea on dry ground'" (Exodus 14:15-16).

Any of you who grew up in church probably know the rest of the biblical story. God split the Red Sea, the Israelites marched through, and the army followed—only to have the walls of water collapse back on Pharaoh's chariots. What you probably have never heard, though, is the role that Nahshon played in the Israelites' escape.

While it's not part of the Bible, the ancient Jewish Midrash commentaries were often attached to the scriptures by rabbis and passed down to new generations. We have Midrash writings that are thousands of years old. There is a teaching around the role of Nahshon that is included in the Midrash on the exodus story. As the story goes, before God would separate the sea, the Israelites had to start marching through it. God wanted them to trust enough to be willing to wade out into the water for themselves. Of course the risk was great. The water could have swept them away, and they could have drowned. Or they could have found themselves immobilized at the exact time that Pharaoh's army arrived on the scene.

Think about this predicament for a minute. Who had ever heard of an entire sea parting? I mean, it is one thing to trust God; it is another thing to walk out into the sea expecting such an outlandish miracle. It seems much safer and much wiser to wait for God to part the sea *first* and then the people can safely walk through. Walking into the water first is risky. After all, what if the water never parts?

So imagine this stalemate between God and the people. God says, "Get in the water, and I will part the sea," while the people say, "Part the sea, and then we will get into the water." Neither side relents; meanwhile Pharaoh's army is getting closer and closer. It's sort of like what Indiana Jones faced in the cave. The people of Israel are running out of time, and it is now or never. Finally, Nahshon decides to step forward in faith.

I want to know where I am going, what it will be like, and where I will end up before I leave behind something certain, safe, and comfortable. But this is not the way God works.

So according to the Midrash, Nahshon, the leader of the tribe of Judah, stepped into the roiling waters. He got his feet wet, but the water didn't part. He went in up to his knees, but still nothing. The water hit his waist, and it went nowhere. Then the water went up to his chest, pushing on him and threatening to pull him offshore with the current. But still God did nothing. Finally, Nahshon waded so deep that the water reached his neck. Any further, and he would go under. It is then, when the water threatened to swallow him, when he was literally neck deep, that God showed up. God invited Moses to raise his staff. Then, and only then, did God take the sea and pull it back, creating walls of water so the Israelites could pass between them and reach the other side.

God was faithful to God's promise. He saved the Israelites and destroyed Pharaoh's army. God made a way when there was no way and created a path through an impossible situation. But according to the commentary, God didn't do it until the people did their part. God didn't show up until Nahshon demonstrated trust and faith by stepping away from shore and out into the sea. As with Indiana Jones, it was only when Nahshon was faithful enough to take the step that God revealed the path forward.

A LAND GOD WILL SHOW YOU

Here is how I wish change would happen in my own life. I wish God would show me where I am meant to go, and *then* I could step away from where I am. As I am a planner, this makes so much more sense to me. Why would you abandon your old life, or dramatically change something, unless you knew where you would end up? That seems crazy.

Let's take a work example, because I know a lot of people who aren't completely satisfied with their jobs. My friend Greg worked for years in a finance job that he didn't like. Actually, to say he disliked it is an understatement. He didn't feel connected to the company's mission, his boss was not a person of integrity, and he didn't like the people he worked with. He felt underappreciated and didn't believe that he was contributing to anything that mattered. He really was unhappy and didn't want to work there. That part isn't all that surprising. Sometimes we just don't connect with a particular workplace. But here was the surprising thing: after feeling this way relatively early on in his time at the company, he continued to work there for more than a decade. Ten years! That is a long time to be unhappy.

When he finally came to me to talk about it, it had been so long that he was almost resigned to the idea that he wasn't going to find anything else he could do. I asked him a very simple question, "Why do you work there?"

He shared with me that, while the list of things he disliked was long, there were also some upsides. Greg was well paid; in fact, his salary was well above average for his field. He had flexibility. And most of all, he had been there so long he knew exactly what he was doing. The job was predictable, secure, and comfortable. Sounds like a definition of home!

So I asked a follow-up question: "Given that you don't like this situation, what would it actually take for you to leave?"

His answer was not surprising. He said, "I have been searching for years for a new job. I have been trying to find a comparable job in the same field that pays the same amount of money. Thus far I haven't found it. The jobs are either outside my field of expertise or don't pay nearly enough. So I am staying until I find the perfect opportunity."

Now, many of you reading this might be thinking to yourself, "I get it, and the approach sounds pretty reasonable. Why step away from a sure thing until you have something else lined up?" Many financial advisors and career coaches would perhaps say the same thing. So what is wrong with this picture?

Well, nothing. In an ideal world, this is exactly how change would work. We would figure out where we are going next, we would know the job description, we would get the offer letter, we would plan our new commute, and we would feel confident that our new coworkers are people we will like. We would have the opportunity to meet our new boss, clarify expectations, and confirm that it is all a good fit. And only then, after all that is done, would we put in our two weeks' notice, leave our old job, maybe take a little vacation, and then start something new. That is how most of us wish change would happen. And every once in a while it does. But most of the time it doesn't. And in my faith life, I have found out that this is almost never the way God works.

My friend made perfect sense. He didn't want to step away from one thing until he knew he had a new thing secured. He didn't want to risk much. He wanted to stay in the same field (he didn't want to start over learning something new). He wanted the same pay (he didn't want to sacrifice anything for the opportunity to make a change). He wanted the same job with the same level of responsibility (he didn't want to give up the seniority he had earned and established). In other words, he wanted a change but wanted the change to have the same benefits, comfort, and safety of home that he already had. And he wasn't going to leave until he knew where he was going. My friend finally realized something about himself: he wanted change without the change.

It sounds silly as I write it out, but I get it. I often want to follow a new nudge, move in a new direction, or change something in my life, but I want to do it without the risk inherent in change. I want to know where I am going, what it will be like, and where I will end up before I leave behind something certain, safe, and comfortable. But this is not the way God works. I constantly have to remember God's words to Abram: "Leave your land, your family, and your father's household for the land that I will show you" (Genesis 1:12).

---

*I knew that the only way I was
going to figure out where this nudge
would lead was to let go, step out,
and follow.*

In these moments, I remember Moses at the Red Sea and the Midrash story about Nahshon. And no matter how I would like change to work in my life, it doesn't usually happen without significant steps that God has led me to take before the waters part and I see a clear way to go forward. I find that I have often had to step away from one thing before God would show me where I was headed. I had to demonstrate trust—something first established by trusting God's promise to lead me and guide me without knowing exactly where the leading and guiding would land me. I have begun to see that stepping out without knowing where my foot will land is the very essence of faith.

At age twenty-four I graduated from Emory University's Candler School of Theology. I was appointed to be an associate pastor in St. Louis, less than an hour from where I grew up. Everything about this seemed ideal to me. I went to college in St. Louis, so I was familiar with the city. My wife and I had just welcomed our first son, so moving close to family felt so much better than being hundreds of miles away. The job was very much like a position I had at a church in Atlanta, so I knew the ropes and what would be expected of me. I felt competent and prepared for what I would be asked to do. I didn't have to worry about where to live because we lived in the parsonage right next door to the church (I didn't yet know the perils of living directly next door to where you work). It was a beautiful neighborhood, one that we never could have afforded to live in had it not been for the church-provided housing. On top of it all, I was the associate pastor, which meant that I was not ultimately responsible for anything. I had the space to learn, to experiment, and even to make some mistakes (within reason), while there were others there to teach and support me. It was great! It felt like I was returning home to a position that, while new, also offered a lot of familiarity. In many ways, it was a dream job, especially for someone right out of school. Once I had it, I imagined holding on to it for a really long time.

But God had other plans for me. After just a year in the position, I had a sinking feeling that, even though everything seemed great, this was not going to be a long-term position for me. It wasn't that anything was wrong with the church.

But I began to notice that most of my twentysomething friends were not going to church. And even though I worked at a church, friends in my age group were largely uninterested in what our church (and most churches) had to offer. They weren't exactly mad at the church; they were just indifferent toward it. They didn't see it as relevant to the lives they were living and the questions they were asking. But here was the irony, at least to me. While my friends were largely uninterested in church, they actually were wrestling with deeply spiritual questions. They would not have labeled them as such. But the questions were ones like:

> What do I want to do with my life?
> What kind of person do I want to be?
> What do I value and want to work for in the
>   world?
> Why am I here, and what difference am I
>   supposed to make?

The list could go on with these kinds of deep, substantive questions. You know what was sad, though? They were asking and trying to answer these questions all by themselves. They didn't have people to talk with or any outside wisdom to guide or challenge their own (limited) thinking. They were doing it all alone.

But here is the beautiful thing. The gospel has so much to say about these questions. I began to sense a call within me to connect the good news taught and embodied by Jesus with my friends who probably weren't going to darken the doors of my church. So I just started inviting people to a small group in my living room. The group gained steam, and by the time I had been there two years, there were twenty to thirty people meeting in my living room for Bible study each week. Then the dangerous stuff happened. I began to sense that the church wasn't connecting with new generations. And I began to get the feeling that maybe God was calling me to do something about it. Maybe I was supposed to start a church that would create Christian community for new generations of people, the kind of people whom most churches have trouble connecting with.

God never promises us change without risk. But what God does promise us, if we are willing to trust, is that God will lead us.

At first I fiercely resisted this nudge. Why? Because I knew nothing about starting a church. I had no idea how to raise money, find a building, and get people to show up. I had never preached every week, managed church finances, or run a board meeting. I had no clue what I was doing. Plus, if I actually tried to start a new church, there would be all sorts of things I would have to give up. No more church-owned house in a good neighborhood. No more paycheck that reliably arrived every two weeks. No more established groups, rituals, and practices that I could plug into and begin to serve. I knew how to be an associate pastor, and

I knew I was good at it. I was comfortable and happy. I had an enviable position at a stable church. I would have to leave behind nearly all of this if I tried to start up something all by myself. (Of course, I wasn't going to be doing it all by myself! God was going with me on the journey. It was all too easy to forget that as I looked back on what I would be leaving behind.)

But God didn't let up. Instead, God's initial nudge turned into a shove. I began to feel strongly that God was calling me to step out and try something that felt risky. I believed that God was calling me, at twenty-seven years old, to start a new church. And I spent a year praying, thinking, talking to trusted people, and trying to get a sense of what this would look like. You have to understand: I am a planner. I wanted to know what I was getting into, what the risks would be, and how to ensure that this new venture would be successful. And yet a whole year of planning, thinking, consulting, and learning did not make the risk go away. It began to dawn on me that no amount of time, no amount of money, and no amount of thinking or praying was going to give me a clear picture of what this new venture would be. It was truly the land that God would show me, and, like Abram, I wouldn't know what it looked like until I let God lead me there. Sure, I could mitigate certain risks, but I could not eliminate the risks. I could not get rid of the scariest part of this whole change: the sheer uncertainty.

I knew that the only way I was going to figure out where this nudge would lead was to let go, step out, and follow. I was going to have to move out of our house without the certainty that I would be able to afford my own place. I was going to have to live with a pay cut—and with no idea how long the cut might last. I was going to have to leave behind what I was good at, with no certainty that I would be good at what was ahead. I had two kids and a wife, and I was not sure that I would be able to provide for them financially in the way I wanted to. I had to leave a sure thing. I had to make a leap, and I didn't know where my feet would land.

It is easy to look back now, with the benefit of knowing the rest of the story. It is easy to forget the fear, the resistance, the hesitancy, and all the times that I almost convinced myself to just stay put. It's easy now to forget that I had never been so scared about anything in my entire life. Period. And all I wanted was to know where God would lead me and what the result was going to be. I just wanted God to assure me that everything was going to work out. I wanted to follow without really forfeiting the sense of "home" that I had created. But that is not the way God works, at least not with me. God's command was simple. Get up and follow me. That's it. Do that *first*. Be obedient in that. Trust that I am not leading you astray or setting you up for failure. Leave first, and then I will take you to a land that I will show you. But I won't reveal what's around the next bend in the path until you lift up your feet and step away. So with fear, uncertainty, and trepidation, I stepped out.

YOUR TURN

I share my story to say that this is what it looked like for me. But the contours and themes of the story are not unique to me. Abram had to leave home not knowing where he was going. Moses left his family and home to go back to Egypt, not knowing how it would turn out. The people of Israel were called to a promised land of milk and honey but had to leave their home in Egypt, not knowing what the journey ahead held for them. All of them had to leave their old situation with no guarantee of what the new situation would look like. All of them had to trust the One who did the nudging and calling. None of them could rely on their own plans, their own risk-management strategies, or their own capacity to control all variables. Instead, the change required them to trust God to lead.

It is almost as if God wants the first part of any journey to be less focused on the destination, or even the map, and more focused on learning dependence and trust. We must learn that if we want to do life with God we have to let go first. Let go of fear. Let go of the need to control. Let go of our obsession with what is safe. Let go of our selfishness. Let go of all the scripts that run in our head about why staying put is better than risking it.

You are going to face this. Some of you already have. You could write your own story about what leaving "home" looked like for you. What did home represent? What did you have to give up? What uncertainties did you have to risk? Many of you can recognize your story in these stories. Some of you are actively considering a change right now, and these feelings are coursing through you even as you read. Life feels turbulent, and the decisions you have to make seem overwhelming. For some of you, things are pretty comfortable. Life may be stable, and you may be settling in to a good place. But wherever you are, know this: there are going to be moments when you are faced with the decision to change, to move, and to embrace something new. Sometimes those moments come by choice; often, however, they just happen to us. All the same, we will face the opportunity to migrate and move from where we are to somewhere new. And many times a tension will arise: it is the feeling that you want to leave, you need to step out, and you are ready to risk, yet you are uncertain of what you are stepping toward.

If God had revealed the trust needed, the sacrifice required, and the risks that the trip to the promised land would entail, the Israelites very likely would have remained slaves.

Don't misunderstand what I am saying. I am not suggesting that we should have blind faith, that we hastily step out every time we sense a nudge, that we take risks that could threaten so much of what is good in our lives without the benefit of counsel and careful consideration. We *ought* to prepare, plan, study, pray, and consult. We ought to do all we can to recognize what change will cost us and then mitigate as much as possible the risks associated with the steps we want to take.

What I am suggesting is this: after all the weeks, months, or sometimes years of discerning, planning, and preparing, you still cannot eliminate all the risks. You never will know *for sure*. In the end, you have to take that leap of faith. You have to step away from one thing, not knowing exactly where you will land. At some point, you just have to leave, trusting that God is going to reveal in due time where you are headed. Like Nahshon, sometimes you are going to have to step into the water, and maybe even get up to your neck in it, before God parts the sea and shows you the next leg of the journey. It will look crazy, and it will be risky, but you also won't be the first one to face it. You won't be last one. You can do it. You *will* do it. You've got this. You were made for this, remember?

Let me leave you with an image that gives me comfort anytime I am faced with a change that requires me to trust. As the Israelites were preparing to leave Egypt, the only home they had ever known, God didn't tell them where exactly they were going or how long it would take to get there. But God didn't leave them alone. As they began their journey, God did something striking and rather curious. Exodus tells us that just as the Israelites were leaving home, God showed up: "The LORD went in front of them during the day in a column of cloud to guide them and at night in a column of lightning to give them light. This way they could travel during the day and at night. The column of cloud during the day and the column of lightning at night never left its place in front of the people" (Exodus 13:21-22).

God never promises us change without risk. God

never promises us a clear road map of what the future will hold. God doesn't promise us that change will not require hardship, sacrifice, and grieving. Letting go always includes those things. But what God does promise us, if we are willing to trust, is that God will lead us. The whole point of not knowing where the path will go is that we *don't have to know*. The reason God didn't tell Abram where they were going is because Abram didn't need to know. God is effectively saying, "If you trust, I'll lead. And as I lead, you just follow."

Israel would end up wandering around the wilderness for forty years before entering the promised land (more on that later). Forty years! It took them that long to learn to trust in God. But every single minute of every single day, God was leading them. A pillar of cloud would lead the way during the day, and a pillar of light would guide them at night. In a place where food and water were scarce, God provided water to drink and food to sustain them. God's promise was that if we do the trusting, God will do the leading. The same promise applies to you.

Right now, God is not asking you to know the future. God isn't asking you to be in control of all potential outcomes. God is not asking you to possess all the necessary capabilities to complete the journey. God is asking you to trust God enough to leave and step out. God is asking you for the first step. Then, and only then, will God lead because then and only then have we given up our own need to know and lead all by ourselves. Trust unlocks the door to the next stage of the journey. Trust parts the sea. Trust reveals the path. God doesn't promise us a road map, but God does promise us guidance for the next step.

Why does it work this way? I have often wondered that, and ultimately, I don't know. But I think Jesus gives us a clue. At the last meal he shared with his disciples, he began to hint at why we rarely get the whole picture from God and instead are asked to just take the next faithful step, trusting that God will reveal more to us as we move. During that last supper, Jesus took the opportunity to share the most important aspects of his ministry. He gave the disciples a new commandment centered on love. He prayed for them, outlined his hopes for them, and looked ahead to the future. During that conversation, almost as if he wanted to share everything, but knowing that his time was limited, Jesus said this: "I have much more to say to you, but you can't handle it now. However, when the Spirit of Truth comes, he will guide you in all truth. He won't speak on his own, but will say whatever he hears and will proclaim to you what is to come" (John 16:12-13).

Jesus essentially said, "*I know* what the future holds for you, but I am not going to share it all with you now. If you were to see it all at once, it is more than you could handle. In fact, you likely would never step out if you knew the road ahead! But I will *guide you*, you will get through it, and I will lead you to something better. But we will do it step-by-step and day-by-day. It is better this way."

I don't like this aspect of God. I'll just admit it. I wish that God would show me the land where I am going. I like to weigh my options. I like to minimize risk and maximize possibilities for success. And I don't like flying blind. I want to know what lies ahead so that I can make the most informed and best decision about whether or not to proceed.

But I also know that the words of Jesus are true and have been true in my life. As I look back at those early decisions—to go to seminary, to start a new church, and even to have kids—if I had seen everything those decisions would entail all at once, I very well may have not taken the steps. If I knew ahead of time everything that ministry entailed, or everything that parenthood entailed, or everything that starting a new church entailed, I might have spent my entire life waiting to get prepared and never actually taking the step.

I suspect the same was true of Abram. If God had told him about the wild adventures that lay ahead, the marital strife, the acts of disobedience, and the pain that he both experienced and caused, he may well have never left home. And yet, had he not left home, he would not have experienced—and been the catalyst for—great transformation. Abram (Abraham) did become the father of many nations, as God had promised, and his act of faith still inspires people today. But it didn't come easily. At the end of his life, I bet Abram was glad he took that step decades earlier. But had the whole thing been revealed to him ahead of time, I think he'd have stayed in Haran.

I suspect the same was true for Moses. If God had shared the whole arc of the journey with Moses at the burning bush, I am fairly convinced Moses would have given God a hard "no." If God had told Moses about the travails of leadership, the moments of despondency, the life-threatening situations, the complaining crowds, do you think Moses would have said yes? I don't. And yet Moses followed God. And because of that, the people followed God from slavery to freedom.

Moses was a witness to countless miracles and to the mighty work of God. He was blessed and is still revered today as one of the greatest leaders and prophets. Moses made his mark on history, and we know that at the end of his life he was glad he followed God's call. But had he known about it all ahead of time, I think he would have remained a shepherd.

We know the same was true for the Israelites. The scriptures tell us, point blank, that they never would have left Egypt, at least not for very long, if God had shown them everything that was in store for them. In fact, they required a significant amount of time in the wilderness, before they could even begin to be ready for the new land that God had prepared for them. If God had revealed the trust needed, the sacrifice required, and the risks that the trip to the promised land would entail, the Israelites very likely would have remained slaves: "I have much more to say to you, but you can't handle it now. However, when the Spirit of Truth comes, he will guide you in all truth. He won't speak on his own, but will say whatever he hears and will proclaim to you what is to come" (John 16:12-13).

I bet the same is true for you. I know it is true for me. God has significant plans ahead for you—plans far beyond anything you could ask for or imagine. But I suspect if you were to know just how difficult the road will be at times, or the challenges that lie ahead, you might stay stuck in the planning stages. Or never leave at all.

So maybe it is God's wisdom that prevents us from being able to see that far down the road, and instead God merely asks us to take the first faithful step. God asks us to leave home for a "land that I will show you." If we do that, God's promise is not that it will be easy, but that God will guide us and provide for us always.

When it comes to a significant change in your life, do your homework, weigh your options, and consider all the risks. But when it comes down to it, remember that you cannot eliminate all the uncertainties, and you can never guarantee success. At some point you have to step out, not knowing exactly where your feet will land. As you do, remember that God will be there with you every step of the way.

Chapter 4

THE ROUNDABOUT WAY

—⟊—

Have you ever driven in a roundabout? In this country (where they're often called traffic circles), you won't find them nearly as frequently as you will find them in Europe and other places around the world. I remember the first time I saw a roundabout. I was a kid watching the movie *National Lampoon's European Vacation*. Forget for a moment that the movie may not have been entirely appropriate for me to be watching as a kid. In the movie there is a scene in which Clark Griswold (Chevy Chase) is driving in London and suddenly enters a roundabout. He has clearly never navigated one before. We can hear him tell his wife that he believes what they should do is just drive around in a circle and then take the second left. As they are rounding the circle, he yells to his kids, "Hey kids, look, it's Big Ben and Parliament," pointing out well-known landmarks on the skyline.

They want to exit the roundabout in order to drive closer to the houses of Parliament. Ellen, Clark's wife, even spots the exit that they should take. The only problem is that Clark is stuck on the inside lane of the roundabout and cannot shift lanes in time to reach the exit. So they go around the roundabout one more time. One more time he yells, "Hey kids, Big Ben and Parliament!" This time, as he tries to shift lanes and exit, a car is blocking his way. They have to go around once again. Pretty soon, we begin laughing because they keep going around and around, never able to get to their exit. Again and again they go right by Big Ben and Parliament without ever reaching them. When the scene ends, darkness has fallen. Clark is still driving around in circles, giddily pointing out Big Ben and Parliament over and over while the family is asleep in the backseat. They of course know where they are trying to drive, but they just can't seem to get there. They seemed destined to spend their vacation riding around the roundabout, never quite getting to where they are trying to go.

I wish that there were a Google Maps app we could access when it comes to navigating change in our lives.

In so many ways this story is symbolic of how it can feel to try to change something significant in your life. You can see so clearly where you want to go. Maybe you even know the path to get there. But actually moving from here to there is more challenging than it first appears, and the route is almost never direct. In fact, it can often feel like a circle, constantly leaving you able to see the change and the new reality, but never quite able to travel there as quickly as you first imagined.

We have talked about the first stage of change, which requires you to leave something behind. That *something*, even if it is unhealthy or painful, is still often familiar. Our current reality is like "home" to us. We know it, we know how to operate in it, it is predictable, and there is a certain comfort and safety in that. As we begin to move toward a new reality in our life, change requires that we leave at least some of that familiarity and predictability behind. Change first requires that we leave home. We see this in the great migration story of scripture, the exodus story. The Israelites and Moses first had to be willing to leave what was familiar. Moses had to leave the comfort of Midian. The Israelites were afraid to leave the familiarity of Egypt even though they were slaves there. Their reluctance shows what a powerful hold security and comfort of the status quo can have on us.

While leaving home is the first hurdle to overcome when we move toward change, it is not the only one. As soon as they left, the Israelites began to experience the next stage of change, and they would spend decades navigating it. Upon leaving Egypt, they immediately realized that before they could get to where they wanted to go, they had to spend time in the wilderness. The wilderness experience is probably the most misunderstood and potentially discouraging part of change.

When the Israelites left Egypt, all they knew is that God had promised them a new land. Specifically, God promised, "I've decided to take you away from the harassment in Egypt to the land of the Canaanites, the Hittites, the Amorites, the

Perizzites, the Hivites, and the Jebusites, a land full of milk and honey" (Exodus 3:17).

They didn't know exactly where this land of milk and honey was. Their ancestors Abraham, Isaac, and Jacob had lived there, but that had been hundreds of years earlier. They didn't know what the journey in getting there would look like or the obstacles they would face. Most important, they had no idea how long it would take them to enter this new land. They were leaving one place without knowing exactly what would come next. And while they perhaps didn't understand it, this in-between space—this gap between leaving one thing and receiving another—would be more challenging than they could imagine. But the in-between space, *after leaving* Egypt and *before entering* the promised land, was no accident. The Israelites weren't lost. God had not abandoned them. And even though they could not see it, they were heading somewhere. All of this was for a purpose—God's purpose. The time in between was designed for a reason, and the Israelites were about to learn that reason.

I raise this now because, if there is only one thing that I want you to remember from reading this book, it is this: just as the Israelites had to spend time in the wilderness, so will you. The wilderness is not an accident. Wandering is not a sign that you made a mistake. God has not abandoned you. While you may have to spend more time there than you ever imagined, there is something on the other side of it. But the wilderness will test you. It will tempt you. It will try to defeat you, and you will be susceptible to giving up, stopping short, or turning around. Don't do it. You aren't alone, and you aren't the first.

The wilderness is hard, but it is necessary. Something important happens there. If you are going to head somewhere new in your life, you are going to have to learn about the wilderness. So let's do it. This section is a guide.

ARE WE THERE YET?

I have three kids, and I have taken my fair share of cross-country road trips with them. There is nothing more memorable or maddening than driving thousands of miles with three kids in the backseat. Any of you who grew up doing it, or have kids of your own, will know the question that is sure to be asked multiple times along the way: "Are we there yet?"

I pestered my parents with it, my kids pester me with it, and I suspect their kids will ask the same question. It is natural. As soon as we hit the road, we would like to know a few basic things. Where are we headed (destination)? How are we going to get there (directions)? And maybe most important, how long is it going to take to get there (timing)? Without answers to these questions, we feel lost. So it is natural for kids to want to know, "Are we there yet?"

Fortunately for my kids, we have Google Maps. Even better, we bought a new vehicle last year. This new car has a handy spot where I can plug in my iPhone and immediately display the map on a big screen for all of them to see. Google Maps is great because in addition to giving you precise directions, it will show you traffic flow, how long you might be stuck if there's a jam, and what alternative routes you might take. It will show you how many miles you have traveled, how many miles you have left to travel, and, most important to my kids, how much time it will take to reach your destination. Thanks to Google, at any given moment along the way, I am ready to answer all the questions about where we are going and how we are going to get there, and to announce, "We've arrived!"

I wish that there were a Google Maps app we could access when it comes to navigating change in our lives. I wish that when I wanted to make a significant change I knew where exactly I was headed, precisely how I was going to get there, and how long it would take before the new reality came into view. I would pay top dollar for an app that could tell me those things. But we don't have that. And neither did the Israelites. Instead they had a leader, Moses, and a God who promised to lead them.

Besides, God doesn't work like Google Maps. God doesn't always pick the most direct route between here and there. God doesn't always tell you exactly which route you are going to take. And God doesn't give you a precise arrival time (or even a ballpark estimate). With God, the destination is not the only important consideration. There is something transformative about the journey.

At the beginning of the Israelites' journey out of Egypt, God provided a sneak peak of the plan. It was a rare moment when God lets us into God's mind and gives us a sense of how God works. I love this scripture. It is just a short passage, but it has spoken to me over and over again. The message is easy to miss, but it is critical: "When Pharaoh let the people go, God didn't lead them by way of the land of the Philistines, even though that was the shorter route. God thought, If the people have to fight and face war, they will run back to Egypt. So God led the people by the roundabout way of the Reed Sea desert" (Exodus 13:17-18).

In case you are not an expert on biblical geography, let me give you a picture of what is going on here. You won't even need to look at a map. Just take your left hand, and look at your palm. See your thumb? That is roughly Egypt. Now look at the tip of your pinky. That is approximately where the promised land is. Now, if you were going to travel from your thumb to the tip of your finger, what route would you take? It's obvious: you would go right across your palm in a straight line. With the pointer finger of your right hand, trace that line from your thumb to your pinky. That course makes sense. It made sense to the Israelites, too. In fact, it is the route that had been used by travelers between Egypt and the land of Canaan for centuries—a route that took them through the northern part of the Sinai Peninsula and stayed close to the coast of the Mediterranean Sea. (No doubt, it is the same route that Joseph's brothers took when they traveled to and from Egypt and eventually brought their families to settle there.) That direct line is roughly "the way of the Philistines" that the passage from Exodus mentions. It went right through the land that the Philistines occupied.

The scripture says God could have taken them that way, which was the most efficient and direct way. But that is not what God did. Instead, God took them through a pretty inhospitable desert, where food and water were hard to come by.

I love that the Bible puts it like this: God led the Israelites along the "roundabout way." Do you know what the roundabout way is? Well, you can get out your "palm map" again and take a look. Put the pointer finger of your right hand at the base of your left thumb. Remember the direct route you drew to your pinky finger. Instead of going that way, just take your pointer finger and start making circles on your palm. That is the roundabout way. God basically says, "I am going to take you in a bunch of circles, around and around. We will move forward, then back to where we started, then forward again. I could take you directly to this new, beautiful land, but not yet. I think that this is the best route."

And there's one other thing God doesn't tell the Israelites yet: it's going to take a lot longer than they think. In fact, it's going to take forty years.

The roundabout way is a route that only God could choose. I have to tell you that, the first time I read this wilderness story, I didn't know whether to laugh or cry. I wanted to laugh because it is funny. It shows God purposefully leading the Israelites around in circles. But I didn't laugh. You know why? Because I get it. I know what it is like to imagine a change in my life, to be able to see where I am and where I want to go. In my mind, it seems like I should be able to get there. Whether during difficult points in my marriage, my raising of kids, or my work in the church, I could often see where I was and where I needed or wanted to be. And it *seems* like I should just be able to go from here to there, to change things easily, cleanly, and quickly. And yet I can't. I can't seem to get there. I can't seem to change things. I cannot easily get from the imperfect place where I am to that ideal place that I can see in my mind. It always takes longer, is less direct, and requires overcoming more obstacles than I ever imagined. In fact, sometimes it seems that I am just running in deep sand, that I can never get to where I am trying to go. The promised land is right over there. I can see it. But I can't get there. I want God to take me "the way of the Philistines," but instead God is taking me the roundabout way. It makes me laugh and cry, all at the same time.

If you know the story, you know it took the Israelites a long time to get to where they were going. You know that they had to spend forty years in that in-between space, what scripture calls *the wilderness*. They had to spend forty years wandering, searching, learning, growing, and doubting before they got to enter the land that God had promised them. The wilderness was not fast, it wasn't easy, and it wasn't accidental. The wilderness served a purpose.

And it isn't just the Israelites of the exodus who had to deal with the wilderness. Their journey is the journey of every person who decides to step out, follow a call, make a change, or take a risk. It is not too much to say that learning to live in the wilderness is key to following through on change in your life. The journey from here to there is never direct, it is never immediate, and it is rarely quick. Usually,

God does not lead us from here to there by the "way of the Philistines." Instead, God takes us the roundabout way. The wilderness is a fundamental feature of migrating and moving, of stepping out and following, not just for the Israelites but for all of us.

This isn't just my hunch. Scripture shows us this truth. In fact, the wilderness pops up time and time again throughout the story of God's relationships with human beings in the Bible. Many centuries after the exodus, for example, the future King David had to flee to the wilderness when King Saul became jealous of him (1 Samuel 23:25). He had to spend his time there, often hiding or on the run, before moving into the new role that God had chosen him for. It was to the wilderness that the prophet Elijah had to flee when he was escaping the anger of the King Ahab and Queen Jezebel (1 Kings 19:4). He wound up at Mount Horeb (Sinai), where Moses also had encountered God, and he was in the wilderness for forty days and nights. Even Jesus spent forty days and nights in the wilderness, experiencing temptation and determining what kind of messiah he was going to be, before he was ready to begin his public ministry (Mark 1). After his experience of encountering Jesus on the road to Damascus and before he began his Spirit-led work of sharing the good news, the apostle Paul had to spend three years in the wilderness (Galatians 1:17-18). In their wilderness experience, the children of Israel had plenty of company. And they still do. All of us will spend time in the wilderness.

WE ALL HAVE A WILDERNESS

My wilderness experience came at an unexpected time. As I was serving as an assistant pastor in a church in St. Louis, I began to feel this nudge to start a new church. I have described the resistance and fear I felt as I stepped away from a real job with a steady paycheck and stepped into this completely unknown thing. But in the spring of 2006, that is exactly what I did. With my wife and two young children, I moved out of the church-owned house that I had lived in, bought my own house (the bank never should have given me a loan), and followed that call to try to do something I had no experience ever doing: starting a church. I remember that, when I finally made the decision, there was this initial rush of excitement. I had a feeling of freedom. I was embarking on an adventure. I wonder if that is what the Israelites felt as they emerged on the other side of the Red Sea. Anyway, to my surprise, that feeling quickly dissipated.

I remember the day that I discovered the seriousness of what I had gotten myself into. It was during my first full week on this new "job." I put *job* in quotes because I was a pastor, and yet I had no church. I was appointed to start one. Earlier that month, an old United Methodist church in the city of St. Louis had to close. After 120 years, that congregation (Immanuel United Methodist) had shrunk to fewer than twelve people, all over the age of seventy. They simply could no longer afford to keep the building open, nor did they have the means and resources to continue their mission. After more than a century on their block in the city, they closed their doors. The old red brick church building with stained glass and a bell tower was slated to be listed and sold, most likely to a developer.

I had driven by the building earlier in the summer. I knew that in just a few weeks I would finally have to do what I had said I wanted to do—start something new. But by now the fear was setting in. There was the fear of having a new mortgage on a house without knowing if I would have a paycheck. The fear of not knowing if I was being responsible enough to support my family. The fear of trying something that I had no idea how to do. The fear of failing when I wasn't used to failing. The fear of looking silly and stupid, confirming the advice that many shared with me *not* to do this. Looking back, there was so much fear. It was pervasive.

Maybe it was out of that fear, or maybe it was because of the Holy Spirit, but I remember driving by that newly closed church. I parked my car, I got out, and I stood outside on the corner of the block. And, standing there, I decided this had to be the place where I started this new church. So the next week, I drove to see my bishop and the decision makers in The United Methodist Church, and I asked them to give me that old building instead of selling it. Pastor friends of mine begged me not to do it.

"Why would you want a church building that people have been driving by and ignoring since the invention of the automobile?" one friend said to me.

I didn't know, except to say that since I had no church, no people, no name, no money, and no real job, getting a building seemed like progress, even if the basement walls were crumbling. I couldn't give a reasonable-sounding answer. But against all advice, I received the keys to that old, abandoned building, and on July 1, 2006, I began my first day there, with the task of figuring out how to start a church inside of it.

Maybe our time in the wilderness is meant to teach us to trust in God, and not just in ourselves, to lead us to the land of promise.

That brings me to the moment during the first week that all of it hit me: the overwhelming nature of the task ahead of me, the completely unknown nature of the journey, the feeling that failure was almost a foregone conclusion. All of it happened as I ate a sandwich while sitting in an old office inside that decrepit building. I don't remember what I did in the morning, but I remember eating that sandwich at an old desk that still had artifacts from a church office that looked like it was set up in the early 1940s. As I finished my meal, I crumpled up the sandwich wrapper and threw it in an old tin trash can sitting in the corner. As it landed at the bottom, I thought to myself, *I wonder what happens to trash around here? I mean, that trash is going to sit in there, and it is eventually going to smell. And there is no one here to take it out. So what will happen?*

So I took the trash can and walked to the basement

kitchen. Down there was a much larger, kitchen-size trash can. I dumped my trash in there and began to walk upstairs when the same thought crossed my mind again: *Matt, there is no one who is going to empty that trash.*

So I went back, I grabbed the larger trash can, and I went outside looking for a dumpster. But there was no dumpster. Then I thought to myself, *I wonder who is going to find a dumpster so that we have a place to throw away trash.* I looked around, and there was no one. So on my first day in a "job" that I was utterly unqualified for, I spent the afternoon calling dumpster companies, learning about the sizes and pickup schedules of commercial dumpsters, and ordering a can to be delivered to our parking lot. And it happened all because I needed to throw away a sandwich wrapper.

At the end of the day, when I thought about that little string of events, it dawned on me that *everything* at this old church was going to be that way. There was no one else to do anything. Everything would have to be created from the ground up. And then it hit me that I was utterly alone. I had set out to do something risky but that I had believed was God-inspired. I had mustered the courage to take the risk, make the decision, and step out. I had mistakenly thought that, once I did that, the hard part was over. I thought that surely God would reward my willingness to listen and follow. God would certainly start to show me the vision that until then I had only seen in my head and heard promised in prayer. I thought that, as soon as I was faithful to move, change, and go, God would immediately show me where we were headed and allow me to begin experiencing the new thing. But in that instant of utter loneliness and isolation I realized it wasn't going to be that easy. There was going to be some in-between time (and maybe a lot of in-between time). That was the day that I began what would be a wilderness journey of many years. I didn't know it then, but the "promised land" was still a ways away. God could have taken me the direct route. There were many times along the journey when I wished God had done that. But God didn't. God was going to take me the roundabout way. And I was going to have to learn the lessons of the wilderness.

THE QUESTION WE ALL ASK

In the stories from the Bible, and in our own lives, we can see that God takes people on the indirect path. We all wonder why. If God calls people to move, change, grow, and take risks; if God asks people to leave home, to head out to unknown places; if God asks people to have faith, take courage, and trust, then why would God reward such faithfulness with what seems like a cruel joke? Why would God purposefully take people in circles, wandering around their own private wilderness until the time when God sees fit? Why wouldn't God want to lead us by the shortest route to where God wants us to be? Why would God lead via the roundabout way? It is a question I have long wondered about, and I think I finally have an answer.

A clue is actually right there in that same scripture passage we looked at earlier: "When Pharaoh let the people go, God didn't lead them by way of the land of the Philistines, even though that was the shorter route. God thought, If the people have to fight and face war, they will run back to Egypt. So God led the people by the roundabout way of the Reed Sea desert" (Exodus 13:17-18).

Did you catch it? Why didn't God lead them by the way of the land of the Philistines, even though that was the shorter route? Here's one reason: God thought, *What if they have to fight and face war?* And God already knew the answer to that question. The easier route actually would have been incredibly hard. The Israelites would have faced too many challenges, and the obstacles would have been overwhelming. The Philistines were strong. Unlike the Israelites, they had iron chariots and iron weapons and well-fortified cities. They were formidable warriors (Goliath, who would menace the Israelites a couple hundred years after the exodus story, was a Philistine). The Philistines would not have let the Israelites pass through their land without a fight. And God knew that the people weren't ready for that challenge yet. In the face of all that, the Israelites likely would have lost their trust in God and in Moses, given up, and headed back to Egypt, even after all they had been through.

God knew that the people needed time—time to learn, time to train, and most of all, time to trust. They needed time before they could proceed to the place that God wanted to lead them. And so instead of taking them by the most efficient and direct route, God took the people through a pretty inhospitable desert, where food and water were hard to come by.

Think for a moment about the implications of that.

God took the people to a place that, instead of offering an abundance of water, was so dry that they would have to depend on God. It gave God an opportunity to use Moses to bring forth water from a rock. God took the people to a place where they couldn't gather enough food on their own to sustain them all; they had to depend on God to provide manna for them to eat. And maybe that was part of the point. In the desert, you become aware of how isolated and vulnerable you are. In the desert, the people had no choice but to trust in God to provide for them. That was the lesson for them and for us. Maybe our time in the wilderness is meant to teach us to trust in God, and not just in ourselves, to lead us to the land of promise.

While the story addresses the journey of the Israelites in the exodus, it actually addresses all of God's people anywhere who choose to listen and follow God's call. All of them (and us) could be led by the shorter route, the way of the land of the Philistines. But God doesn't do that. Why? Because if God did, God knows that most of us would face too much, too fast. We would face obstacles greater than we are currently able to overcome and adversaries who are strong enough to intimidate us into giving up. We aren't ready for that yet. And so God, in God's wisdom, doesn't do that. God takes us the roundabout way. God takes us to the wilderness. And this brings me back to my initial point. It isn't by accident that God takes us there. God does it for a reason.

We are not yet the people God needs us to be. Maybe we're not ready to go to the places that God wants us to go. That is not a pessimistic statement. I don't write it to discourage you. It just means that you aren't yet ready for what it coming. But that is OK. Before God can do something new with us, God has to do something new *in* us. We have to become new people so that we can head to the places that God wants to lead us. The wilderness is rough, but if you allow it, the wilderness can become the most formative part of your journey.

Why is that? It's because the wilderness forces us to understand the reality that we can't do it alone and that we have to put our ultimate trust in God to see us through to the other side.

In spite of all they had seen as God delivered them from Pharaoh's hand, the Israelites hadn't learned to trust fully in God. They accused God of leading them out into the wilderness to die. As we will see, they even gave up on God and made an idol to worship. It would take them four decades of wandering to learn, finally, the lesson of the wilderness: in a barren place where there is no food and little water, they had to put their trust in God to provide what they needed every single day.

The wilderness isn't a cruel, divine joke. The wilderness is a training ground. It is a place for learning, shaping, confronting, growing, and changing. Like any kind of training, the wilderness isn't easy. It wasn't easy for Moses, for the Israelites, for David, or for Elijah (who I'll talk more about in a later chapter).

God uses the wilderness to teach us to trust.

And when we trust, we're no longer on the roundabout

way. We're walking by faith and not by sight. And we can gain the strength that can sustain us through some hard miles that still lie ahead before we cross into the promised land.

You will have wilderness moments in your life. There is always a gap between the places we leave and the places we will end up. Quite often, those wilderness journeys are going to seem unnecessarily long and winding. There are going to be moments when you don't believe you are making any progress at all. The wilderness is a defining feature of your journey, of every journey. Even Jesus's journey. The roundabout way has a purpose, though. Progress is being made, even if you can't see it. Something is happening, and the time will not be wasted. Learn to be OK with wilderness experiences because it is in the wilderness that God is able to do some of God's best work. It is on that roundabout route that we become the people God needs us to be, in order to take us to the place God wants us to go.

Chapter 5

TURNING BACK TO EGYPT

—◦◦◦—

When I was in fifth grade I decided to do something that perhaps many of you did (or at least considered) at some point in your childhood. I decided to run away from home.

I can't remember what great injustice caused me to come to this conclusion. It wasn't because of my parents, who were (and are) great. They were loving, supportive, and present. In fact, as I look back, I think I grew up in the ideal household with the ideal parents. I couldn't have dreamed up something better. But sometimes when you are a kid, it is hard to see that. That day, they must have made some decision that upset me. Whatever it was, that day I decided that I'd had enough. I was going to show them. I could do this all by myself (at least for a day or two). I was going to run away.

I hadn't really thought about this in advance, and if I had, I would have quickly come to the conclusion that running away was an unrealistic idea. After all, I grew up in a small town in rural Missouri. To be more accurate, our house was outside the small town. While we had neighbors, there wasn't much around but farmland and woods. It was ten miles or so to the nearest town. But none of that really mattered to me in that moment. I wanted to make a statement. I didn't have to submit to their unjust treatment of me. I wanted to call their bluff. I wanted to show my parents that I would leave. And so I packed my backpack with a few essentials—a toothbrush, some clothes, a few granola bars, and some water—and I left. It felt great to slam the door and walk out toward freedom! Or so I thought.

The wilderness is a place where God can do something new in us.

It didn't take long before my emotions began to change. After about ten minutes of walking, I was in the middle of nowhere—just farmland and woods. Ten miles or so to the nearest town, I began to question my original decision. This whole leaving home thing sounded like a good idea when I was in the comfort of my bedroom. It felt a whole lot different when I was wandering through the woods and wondering where in the world I was going (and how I was going to get there). It didn't take an hour for me to start running home. By that evening I was back around the dinner table with my family. I am not even sure my parents realized that I had left. If they did, they didn't show it. I suspect they knew what would happen, and they let me figure it out for myself. It was the first time I realized that it is one thing to say you want to leave, but it is another thing to actually do it. And even if you do it, the urge to turn around will arise much faster than you think. At least it did for Moses and the Israelites.

GRUMBLING

Now when I ran away from home, there were some glaring differences between me and the Israelites. I had a great home; they were in slavery. I had nurturing, caring parents; they had taskmasters. I was heading nowhere, while they were on the way to a promised land. There was every incentive for me to turn around and head home after I realized that wandering around in the woods with no particular place to go was not near as nice as a hot meal, warm bed, and Nintendo (and not just any Nintendo either, because this was in the early 1990s, and it was Nintendo Classic!). For me, losing my resolve to keep going and instead turning back toward home made sense. Even though I still thought I would last longer than a couple of hours, even if it just was to make a point. But I didn't achieve either of those.

The surprising thing is that, despite every incentive to keep going, it didn't take the Israelites long before they did the same thing that I did. In fact, the Bible tells us just how long it took them—forty-five days. In just a month and a half into their journey, after witnessing how God raised up Moses to confront Pharaoh, sent the plagues, split the Red Sea, overthrew Egypt's army, and guided them by day and night, after all of this, the Israelites decided that this wilderness stuff was kind of hard. They were hungry. Their feet hurt. They didn't love the food options. They started complaining and ultimately asked to go back home:

> The whole Israelite community set out from Elim and came to the Sin desert, which is located between Elim

and Sinai. They set out on the fifteenth day of the second month after they had left the land of Egypt. The whole Israelite community complained against Moses and Aaron in the desert. The Israelites said to them, "Oh, how we wish that the LORD had just put us to death while we were still in the land of Egypt. There we could sit by the pots cooking meat and eat our fill of bread. Instead, you've brought us out into this desert to starve this whole assembly to death." (Exodus 16:1-3)

Now this was hardly the first time the Israelites had complained, as you may remember from the previous chapters. In fact, they began complaining even before they crossed the Red Sea. Then, just days into the wilderness, they complained that they had nothing to drink. So God gave them water. This represents the first of what would become a wilderness habit for the Israelites. They would see their circumstances, begin to complain or grumble, get nostalgic about their past in Egypt, and then ultimately want to turn around and return to the way things had been before. It is a pattern that is important for us to pay attention to because it represents one of the primary temptations of the wilderness, which is to turn around and head right back where you came from. The wilderness can do that to us, especially when we are not prepared for it or we don't know what to look for. The wilderness is a place where God can do something new in us. But it is also a place of testing and temptation. The first temptation the Israelites had to face— and, by extension, that any of us who listen and follow God have to face—is to turn around and head back.

What is the sign that you are being tested in the wilderness? Well, it usually begins with grumbling and complaining. To illustrate what complaining can do to us and how it can distort our perspective, let me take a different version of this same story. It gives a little more detail, and I love the language. I can picture it. It is from the Book of Numbers: "The riffraff among them had a strong craving. Even the Israelites cried again and said, 'Who will give us meat to eat? We remember the fish we ate in Egypt for free, the cucumbers, the melons, the leeks, the onions, and the garlic. Now our lives are wasting away. There is nothing but manna in front of us'" (Numbers 11:4-6).

Nostalgia is the art of making the past seem better than it really was.

What is going on here? The riffraff (do I have to explain that, or do you get the idea?) started to complain. Why were they complaining? Because they didn't have meat to eat. A month or so earlier, they had complained that they were going to starve. So what did God do? God decided to come and show them just how much God was watching over them. God wanted to show them just how present God really was. God wanted to prove to them that they could trust God's leadership and direction, even if they didn't know where they were going. So how did God do this? God sent them manna. Scripture describes manna as a flaky, white, bread-like wafer with a taste of honey. Every morning (except for the Sabbath), God would send the manna like dew to rest on the ground. (And on the day before the Sabbath, God would provide enough manna for two days.) The food was literally waiting there for the Israelites when they woke up in the morning. All they had to do was get up and step outside their tent, and there it was *right in front of them*! All they would need for the day—their daily bread—would be right there. Talk about a silver platter! No hunting, no searching, no worrying, no anxiety, no starving. Ever. As long as they were in the wilderness, God promised them this manna. The manna sustained them and reminded them that God had their back and that God's provision would be enough to see them through the trials and tribulations of the wilderness.

This makes the Israelites' complaint in Numbers all the more shocking. Not more than a month or so after God did this incredible thing in their lives, they started to grumble again. And do you know what their complaint was? They don't have any meat to go along with this manna. In other words, "Thanks, God, for providing for us every single day so that we never have to worry or grow anxious again, but we don't really love this menu. Can you mix it up a little bit? How about the occasional filet mignon?" This story would be funny if it weren't so painfully true—not just for them, but for all of us.

You could argue that the people complained because they wanted some variety in their diet. Or maybe they were just complainers. But I think the issue is something more basic. It is the reason that any of us ever complain about anything. Somewhere out in the wilderness, the Israelites lost perspective. Their vision got distorted. And here's how. In the wilderness they stopped seeing what they had and started focusing on what they didn't have. Let me say it a different way. They stopped noticing how God was blessing them, providing for them, and protecting them. And they started focusing on what God *wasn't* doing for them, what God wasn't providing, and what God wasn't protecting them from. They stopped noticing the blessing that was literally right in front of them. And instead they started whining and moaning over what they didn't have.

BLIND TO BLESSING

I can remember my first year in ministry at my current church, The Gathering. There were days when I would have my own version of a pity party with God. One example that sticks out occurred the night before we were to have our first practice worship service. I had no idea what I was doing. Since I had never run a church before and had no clear idea what I was doing, I thought it would help to have a practice worship service a couple of months before we had planned to start weekly services. As the date approached, I felt a growing sense of panic. I had no musicians. So I enlisted a band from a neighboring church to come and play. I had no sanctuary (ours was torn up while a small group of volunteers remodeled it). So we set up a temporary worship space in the downstairs fellowship hall (that is church language for basement). I had no money for technology or décor. So we printed off some words on a sheet of paper, and

I borrowed a friend's projector and screen. Since the building we inherited had no air conditioning (and the temperature in July regularly soars above one hundred degrees in St. Louis), we finagled a few window air conditioning units for the space (they didn't provide much relief). I had set out to start a church that was compelling for new generations of people, and this was shaping up to be anything but compelling.

At least that is how I felt the night before that first practice service. I was completely underwhelmed with the sermon that I had written (pastors will know what that feels like). Instead of in a hip, new space, we were going to worship in an old church basement with faux wood paneling, crumbling plaster, uncomfortable mismatched seating, and some not-very-good air-conditioning units. Instead of having a polished and seamless worship experience, we were going to be lucky to have a working projector. On top of it all, I had no idea if anyone would even show up. Then, as if on cue, I received a phone call at about 9:00 p.m. on the night before the service from the band that had volunteered to play. They cancelled. At that point I reached the end of the line. I crumpled up my sermon, threw it in the trash can, and broke down. I began to complain to God. If you could listen inside my head it went something like this: "God, I have done everything that I thought you wanted me to do. I left my old ministry position (a sure thing, by the way, with a paycheck and lovely people). I embarked on this adventure trusting you. I have worked hard, more hours than I should. I have sacrificed time with family and friends. I have tried to be faithful in every way. We set out to start a church that would attract whole new groups of people, sharing the good news that you said you wanted shared. I did all this, and now this is just going to fail before it ever gets started. Here we are with no money, a crappy space, a no-show band, and a bad sermon to boot."

There I was: a twenty-nine-year-old man crying in my family room, throwing my own little pity party in front of God because I thought God had led me out into a wilderness. It felt like everything that I was working for was falling apart. Nothing was going right. My family was put at risk, my financial security felt shaky, my reputation was on the edge of a cliff, and failure seemed inevitable. That is how it *felt*. God had led me away from one thing to have me die in the wilderness. I didn't understand why.

Since then, I have told that story to others, and people tried to console me. "Don't be too hard on yourself, Matt," they would say. "Anyone would have felt the same way you did."

And maybe that is true. But looking back, I made the same mistake the Israelites made. I stopped seeing the signs of blessing that were all around me (and they were there), and I started seeing all the things I didn't have. I stopped seeing the ways God was continuing to bless me, and I started focusing on all the ways that it felt like God *wasn't* blessing me. I stopped seeing that God was protecting my family, that I had a whole denomination supporting me, that there were cheerleaders and prayer warriors all around me. I stopped seeing that I had a team of forty to fifty people who would take a hill with me. I stopped seeing that, amid all my stress and distress, I still had a house in a good neighborhood, healthy kids, a bed to sleep in, and food on my table. I stopped seeing that I had an incredible family, loyal friends, and loads of opportunity. I stopped seeing all the blessings that were right in front of me. Instead, all I could see was what I lacked, what wasn't there. As soon as things got difficult in the wilderness, it began to warp my perspective. I stopped seeing the manna right in front of me every day.

It is so easy for us to do. What can begin as a blessing in our lives becomes routine as time goes by—so much so that we stop seeing it altogether. I bet this is true for you as well. I bet that, in low points, times of frustrations, and seasons when things aren't progressing as you thought or hoped they would, your vision gets warped too. I bet you stop seeing the manna and start focusing on all the ways God (supposedly) isn't showing up for you.

We recognize the "riffraff's" complaint—or at least we should. They stopped seeing the manna that was right in front of them and started focusing on the food they didn't have. And so do we. And that leads to something else: nostalgia for the bad old days.

NOSTALGIA

The dictionary definition of *nostalgia* involves a sentimental longing for the past. I will define it a little bit differently. Nostalgia is the art of making the past seem better than it really was. As a retired pastor told me once, "The good ol' days weren't that good; they were just old."

As soon as the Israelites stopped focusing on the God who had brought them this far, as soon as they stopped seeing the way that God was blessing them and sustaining them, as soon as they stopped seeing the manna as an amazing gift that came to them for their daily sustenance, they did the only thing left to do. When you stop looking forward, you start looking back. The scripture says the Israelites looked back and started to "remember" Egypt.

When we start complaining, we are tempted to make the biggest mistake we can make in the wilderness. We are tempted to turn back.

But what did they remember? Did they remember the slavery? Did they remember the long work days and the oppressive conditions? Did they remember the whips, the chains, and the blood? Did they remember the centuries of prayer begging God to hear their cry and free them? No. As the Bible story tells us: "We remember the fish we ate in Egypt for free, the cucumbers, the melons, the leeks, the onions, and the garlic" (Numbers 11:5).

Really, this scene is almost comical. If would be funny if it weren't so pathetic. The Israelites don't remember any of the things that made life in Egypt unbearable. Instead, they miss the free fish, the cucumbers, the watermelon, the onions, and the garlic. Never mind their enslavement. Never mind that Egypt was painful. Never mind they were stuck. Never mind that they prayed to God asking to be freed. The melons were pretty good, and the fish was free!

Just as their vision was distorted in the wilderness so that they couldn't see the blessing of the manna and could only focus on what they didn't have, so the Israelites looked at the past through that same distorted lens. They remembered none of the challenges and pain. They remembered none of the reasons why they wanted to leave. Suddenly they started remembering selectively. Worse, they started idealizing the past as if it had somehow been better than it really was. They started to get nostalgic. And nostalgia can be the enemy of forward progress.

Now, there's nothing wrong with nostalgia, in its proper place. Most of us have times in our lives on which we can look back with fond memories and sentimental feelings. Maybe that's how you look back on your school days or the times when you first met and were dating your spouse or a time you spent with parents who are no longer living. There's nothing unhealthy about being nostalgic about the past as long as you're living in the present and focused on the future.

But nostalgia can be a dangerous and seductive temptation when we are in the throes of the wilderness because the wilderness distorts our vision. It causes us to trade the potential of the present and promise of the future for a past that is now only a mirage because we can't go back there. And make no mistake: for the Israelites, the past was a mirage. After all, the fish was not free (they were slaves). Something tells me the melons probably weren't that great, either. But when you are wandering in the desert, the uncertainty and fear can cause you to see some strange things.

You can see it in your life, can't you? In one way or another, we have all been where the Israelites were. We get scared in the wilderness, and that makes us see the past as better than it was and blinds us to the potential of the present.

I remembered a conversation I had with a woman in my congregation who was engaged to a guy whom she knew wasn't good for her. The guy didn't treat her well, they fought constantly, they found it tough to see each other's point of view, and (almost needless to say) they didn't seem to be having fun. In a counseling session, I finally said to them, "You seem to be really frustrated with each other. A lot. Why do you want to marry this other person?" Now sometimes a question like that can help you laugh and brush aside nonessentials and focus on the good stuff. But sometimes, the question isn't rhetorical. It is meant to be answered.

I got a phone call a week later, and the woman decided to call off the wedding. It was a painful and difficult decision, but one that she felt God was nudging her to make. I agreed. So she did it. Upon leaving that relationship, she suddenly found herself single again, with everything that being single entails. She entered the wilderness—that time in between where she was and where she would ultimately end up—and she felt a little lost. For a few weeks, it was fine, but pretty soon she hit her first real challenge, which was loneliness. Many of you know what that is like. It is the Friday night when you realize that everyone you know seems to have something to do except for you. It is spending time on Instagram and seeing all the other couples getting engaged, having babies, going on vacation, or just hanging out and having fun. Throw in a few online dates that go awry, and pretty soon you begin to believe that you will never find someone and that you are destined to be alone for the rest of your life. (By the way, if this sounds dramatic to those of you who have been in a relationship a long time, it isn't. Just talk to someone you know who is single.) It is hard.

What was true for the children of Israel is also true for us: the only way through the wilderness is forward.

When the loneliness hit after she called off the wedding, this woman suddenly stopped focusing on moving forward. She forgot why she had left the relationship in the first place. She no longer saw the potential that existed in the present, and she started remembering the past. Except she did what the Israelites did: her memory got fuzzy. In the challenge and loneliness of the wilderness she started remembering the past as a time in her life that was much better than it actually was. Suddenly that dysfunctional relationship didn't seem so bad. At least she had someone. And those fights, they could be worked through. Maybe she just hadn't given it long enough. Maybe it was her fault that the relationship didn't work out. Maybe she needed to try it again. Maybe this time it could be different. In a moment of weakness she talked to me and confessed that maybe she had made a mistake.

And you know what? Maybe she did. But I don't think so. I started reminding her of what it was actually like, what she actually felt, and how hard it was to actually make the bold move to break it off and move forward. She agreed. She decided to stay the course. But misplaced nostalgia is tempting. When we start complaining, when we stop seeing the potential in the present, when we get nostalgic for the good old days that weren't so good, we are tempted to make the biggest mistake we can make in the wilderness. We are tempted to turn back. We are tempted to throw in the towel and head back to Egypt. After all, at least the fish there were free.

TURNING BACK

The story we read above is just one of the many times during their wilderness journey that the Israelites were overcome by the uncertainty of their circumstances, grew nostalgic for their time of slavery in Egypt, and wanted to turn around and go back to Pharaoh. That phrase has become an analogy for all the ways in which the journey toward something new is fraught with the temptation to go back to the way things were, not necessarily because the past was good, but because the past is known and familiar.

When we start growing nostalgic, a couple of things can happen. First, our perspective grows distorted. The change we are making suddenly seems less urgent or needed, and the past seems not so bad in retrospect. When this happens we begin to question our judgments, our choices, and ourselves. We begin to question the wisdom of our decision. Did we really think it through? Did we give the past reality a fair chance? Were we too hard on it or too eager to jump into something new? Maybe we should have stuck it out, taken more time to consider our options, or waited until the timing was more favorable. Maybe we didn't prepare for the wilderness enough or think about the challenges thoroughly enough. Maybe we didn't give the Egyptians enough of a chance to change their behavior. Were we too rash, too quick to leave, too hasty with our decision? The self-doubting and questioning can go on and on and on. Such is the challenge of the wilderness and the effects of misplaced nostalgia.

And here's the thing. Sometimes we have reason to question our decision. Of course it is natural, but sometimes we are hasty, and we are rash. Sometimes we don't think it through. And every once in a while, I guess turning around and going back may be the best option. I don't want to pretend like every time we sense and follow a nudge that it is the right decision. But I do know this: every time we do listen and follow a God-given nudge, we will hit a point in the journey when we will question it and question ourselves. We will hit a point when the past begins to look better than it was and our vision grows dim and seems less clear or compelling than it once was. This is the nature of the journey. It is one of the primary temptations of the wilderness. And usually—not always, but usually—our temptation to turn around is one that it natural, expected, and wrong for us to follow!

Second, nostalgia not only keeps us longing for something that cannot be retrieved (and in many cases never was really there to begin with) but also keeps us from seeing the new paths that God is opening in front of us. Sometimes, our biggest barrier to future possibilities is past memories. Longing for the way things used to be keeps us from seeing the way things *can* be. This happens to us as individuals, but I especially see it as something that often happens in organizations, schools, companies, and churches.

I have the opportunity these days to travel around the country talking to groups of pastors and church leaders. I listen to the stories of struggle and challenge that a lot of churches are experiencing in a world that is rapidly changing all around them. In the midst of all of that change, these churches feel as if they have been thrust into a wilderness that they didn't necessarily choose. They aren't what they used to be, and what they will end up being is not clear. They are traveling, sometimes against their will, from the way things were to the way things will be. And they do not know when they will arrive or even if they will get there successfully. As they try to deal with this new reality, so many churches cannot seem to let go of the way things used to be. Nostalgia keeps them remembering the days when the pews were full, kids roamed the halls, and the offering plates overflowed. They will remember when people used to prioritize church or when the youth group was thriving. Whatever the memory, it is clear they cannot let go of the way things used to be. The problem with this is twofold. First, after some investigating, churches often find that their memory of past glory never was really accurate. (I have often looked back over church statistics to find that the attendance was never quite at the lofty level they remembered!) Second, but more important, trying to recapture an imagined past only keeps churches (or any organization) from actually creating a new future. We only have so much attention, energy, passion, and time to commit. The more time we spend looking backward means the less time that we can spend looking toward the possibilities of the future. There is a huge difference between those churches and individuals who use every bit of their available resources and energy to live into the future and those who waste those same resources bemoaning a lost past.

In many cases (both in church and in life), we can turn back toward Egypt, but in reality there is no Egypt to go back to. Egypt is gone. Think for a moment what would probably have happened if the Israelites had given up and tried to go back to their old lives in Egypt. Do you think that Pharaoh would have welcomed them back after losing his army and after all the plagues that Egypt had suffered? And do you think that the Israelites would have been happy to live again under slavery (assuming Pharaoh would have let them) after they had cried out to God for help for so long and had a taste of freedom? For both questions, the answer is: I doubt it. What was true for the children of Israel is also true for us: the only way through the wilderness is forward.

STAYING FOCUSED

When you find yourself in the wilderness, you will be tempted to turn around. You will stop seeing the blessings around you, start seeing what you don't have, and begin to remember what you left behind. Your vision will get distorted. You will be tempted to give up the journey, to turn around, and to head back to Egypt. Sometimes, going back is possible. Oftentimes, there is no Egypt to return to. Either way, fear and nostalgia can prevent us from seeing the possibilities of a better future. You will experience this. It is *normal*. But when you do face it, you have a choice to make. You can choose to direct your vision and energy to *what you are leaving*, or you can stay focused on *where you are going*. The key to staying the course while in the early stages of the wilderness is to keep focused on where God is leading you and why God is leading you there. Keep at the forefront of your mind the reason you decided to make a change, the promise of the new reality, and the sense that God is doing something in and through you, even though you cannot see it. As the apostle Paul would remind the early Christians of Corinth, Greece, more than a thousand years after the Israelites were led through the wilderness, "We walk by faith, not by sight" (2 Corinthians 5:7 NRSV).

As tempted as the Israelites were to turn back, and as often as they wanted to do it, they never did. Each time the grumbling came, God would show up in a visible and palpable way to keep the Israelites focused on the present and future instead of on the past. God had to constantly keep their eyes focused on where God was *leading* and not what they were *leaving*. The more focused they stayed on the promised land, the less likely they were to turn back toward Egypt.

The same is true in our lives today. We can focus on what is wrong, what's disappointing, what people around us aren't doing, and what isn't working in our lives. We can focus on our challenges, our setbacks, our hardships, and the injustices that we have had to suffer. Day to day, it is easy to get consumed with the immediate concerns of life, the busy schedules, obligations, chores, and to-do lists. It is easy to get distracted from the new life that God is calling us to live and the journey that God is calling us to take. And when we get distracted, it is so easy to start focusing on the past and what we miss, rather than on the future and where we are going.

There is a story in the Gospel of Matthew that illustrates this well. The disciples were on a boat crossing the sea of Galilee when a storm kicked up. The waves were crashing against the boat, it was dark, and the disciples couldn't see the shore. Most of all, they felt alone. Jesus was not in the boat with them. Suddenly, they saw a figure walking on water. They thought it was a ghost, but of course it was Jesus. He shouted out to them, speaking words of encouragement. He told them not to be afraid. He wasn't absent, and they weren't alone. But Peter desired proof. He wanted more. So he said to the figure on the water: "Lord, if it's you, order me to come to you on the water."

What happens next is well known. You probably know the story: "And Jesus said, 'Come.' Then Peter got out of the boat and was walking on the water toward Jesus. But when Peter saw the strong wind, he became frightened. As he began to sink, he shouted, 'Lord, rescue me!' Jesus immediately reached out and grabbed him, saying, 'You man of weak faith! Why did you begin to have doubts?'" (Matthew 14:28-31).

In the ancient world, the symbolism of this story would have been understood. The stormy sea was a symbol of the chaos and uncertainty of the universe. The boat was a symbol of safety and security on the stormy sea of life (that is why the boat was an early symbol for the church). But Jesus wasn't in the boat; he was in the chaotic, uncertain, and dangerous water. And he called Peter to join him on a journey away from the boat toward himself: a journey toward Christ, toward faith, toward trust, and toward new life. Peter listened and stepped out, which is one of the more courageous acts of faith in the Gospel. And for a few steps, he was doing well. He was locked in on where he was going and the one who was calling him. But then something happened. He got distracted. He noticed the strong winds and the threatening waves. I suspect he glanced down and saw the sea and probably even looked back to see just how far away from the boat he really was. He stopped noticing that he was in the middle of a miracle, that he was walking on water! Instead, he started noticing all the challenges and all the ways this could go wrong. Peter took his eyes off where he was going; and, more important, he took his eyes off Jesus, who was guiding and calling him. And when he did, he started to sink.

As we take risks to follow Jesus away from the safety of our boat and into uncertain futures, the same thing is going to happen to us. Just as the Israelites stopped seeing their blessings and started focusing on their challenges, you, too, will be tempted to focus on the challenges of the wilderness. Just as Peter stopped seeing the miraculous nature of his journey and started seeing the storm, you, too, will be tempted to see all the reasons why your own journey is doomed. The result for all of us is essentially the same. The Israelites wanted to run back to Egypt; Peter likely wanted to swim back to the boat; and oftentimes we will want to abort the mission and just return to the way life used to be. Change can sound good in the abstract. Taking a bold step to follow God can sound inspiring in a book. But in real life, following God to a new reality can feel more like being lost in the wilderness or sinking in a stormy sea. We will experience the fear that Peter felt. We may ask, like Peter and the Israelites did, "What have I gotten myself into? How am I going to get out?" And that opens the door of temptation to take the one route we already know—the route that leads back to Egypt.

And while it can sound cliché, the solution, the antidote, the way we overcome this temptation, is to stay focused on the one calling us. Stay focused on Jesus, his presence in our lives, and where he is calling us to go. We have to stay focused on where God is leading and not on what we are leaving.

I learned this from my own experience. The night before that first trial-run worship service, when I was crying in the family room of my house, I had a choice. And believe me, I was so tempted to just quit. To say, "Forget this. I am not starting a new church and risking all of this." It hadn't been that long, and I had just started out on my journey. I hadn't come that far from the boat. Egypt wasn't too far away. It wasn't too late for me to say, "Never mind." I could have pretended that I was just considering a new journey in faith and that I had reconsidered. Besides, the "Egypt" I'd have returned to wasn't slavery and brutality; it was a secure job with a defined job description and a stable paycheck, in a position of service to God and the church. Believe me when I tell you that the temptation was so real for me, I almost did it. I almost went back.

But by the grace of God I didn't. And I really mean that it was by the grace of God. I sat there, crying in my family room, for about twenty minutes. And then, as if God were physically in the room, I felt like a hand was patting me on the back, challenging me to dry my eyes and stop the pity party. It felt to me like God was saying, "Enough, Matt. Stop doubting. Stop feeling sorry for yourself, and stop giving up. Refocus. Look at me. Trust me. We've got this."

Ultimately, as trite as that might sound, it was true. On my own, I would have given up that night. I am convinced of that. I am too scared of failure and like to play it too safe to have continued. I am convinced that, on their own, the

Israelites would have run back to Egypt, begging Pharaoh's forgiveness and settling back in to a life of garlic and melons and not-so-free fish. On his own, Peter would have continued sinking in the Sea of Galilee, and he likely would have drowned in the storm. But I wasn't alone. The Israelites weren't alone. Peter wasn't alone. And neither are you.

Maybe you are up against some pretty big challenges right now. Maybe self-doubt and fear are crashing in on you like waves battering your small boat. Maybe you are questioning everything about your journey and what you thought God was calling you to do. But take it from some experienced wilderness wanderers. Stay focused. Don't get distracted. Don't look up at the wind or down at the depth of caverns. Don't focus on the immediate obstacles or the uncertainty of the next day. And whatever you do, stop looking back, wondering if maybe, just maybe, it isn't too late to return to the starting point. Instead, remember *why* you started. Remember the urgency you once felt to step out. Remember the sense that God was calling you to something new. Remember that there is a promised land waiting for you. Most of all, stay focused on Jesus, who is present with you, guiding you, leading you, giving you courage, and taking your hand when you begin to fall.

Chapter 6

THE DIP

—✺—

"Sometimes, things get worse before they get better."

As a math major, I tend to think of things in numerical categories. I geek out on pie charts and graphs. It is just in my nature. I have observed that most people imagine their lives as following a fairly simple mathematical trajectory. In mathematical terms, we believe life should be a y = x kind of equation. For you nonmath folks, I call it an "up and to the right" approach to life. If you were to graph this equation and draw a picture of the way most of us imagine life, it would look something like this:

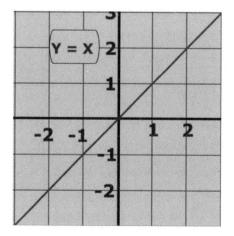

To press the analogy a bit further, we imagine that the older we get and the further along we go in life the better things ought to be. Think about it. When it comes to picturing your career, don't most of us imagine "starting out at the bottom," and then as we get older, smarter, and more confident, we get better and better at our job (along with requisite raises and promotions)? Think about this in financial terms. Most of us imagine starting out with relatively little, and then, over time, as we work and grow up, we gain progressively more. Think about it relationally. We imagine our marriage or even friendships deepening and getting better with time. Emotionally, we imagine that, as we grow up, gain perspective, and mature, we will better deal with stress, anxiety, and uncertainty. When it comes to faith, we imagine each day drawing a little closer to Jesus and becoming a little more the person God calls us to be. We imagine life as "up and to the right"—a long and sometimes slow progression, but always getting better.

Like so many of us, the Israelites expected a life following God to be one of blessing. They did not understand that they would have to trust God to take them through a number of valleys that would be strange and scary.

This is a hopeful way to look at life. Even if we make mistakes and stumble along the way, most of us still imagine that life is actually getting better and each day we are becoming better people. We not only believe it but also assume it and expect it. Some of us even feel like we have a right to this steady progress. Therefore, it feels like a tragic injustice whenever something happens that causes our life to go "backward." We may see it as almost unfair when something takes us back to square one and makes us feel like we are starting all over again. This is just not the way life is supposed to work.

Many of you know this feeling. It is the feeling that comes with getting divorced after twenty-five years of marriage. At a time when your friends are sending kids off to college and anticipating more time together, you are suddenly on Match .com reentering the dating world after a hiatus of several decades. Or it is the feeling that comes after investing heavily in your company and career, expecting and anticipating all that work to earn you promotions and relative security, only to watch helplessly as your company is sold and then to find yourself without a job. It is the feeling that comes when you look around and see friends buying their starter home or "dream home" while you are declaring bankruptcy and preparing to move back in with your parents. It is going to church for years and seeing others thrive and engaged in their faith at a time when you feel as if your faith is slipping and you are wondering if it is all real anyway. It is the feeling that comes as you watch new parents send out joy-filled pictures on Instagram when you have been trying unsuccessfully to become a parent for years. Whatever the situation, I think you know what I am talking about. There are times when life just doesn't develop as we imagined; it doesn't follow the neat, steady, up-and-to-the-right trajectory we expected. At times, it even seems to stall and go backward when everyone else seems to be moving full steam ahead.

These are the moments when it feels like you have hit a low point, a place you never thought you would be in life, a place you never prepared for or expected. It can feel as if God has abandoned you. It can feel like you are failing when everyone around you seems to be moving ahead. We don't plan these moments. We don't predict them. We certainly don't plot them on our graph of what life is going to look like. So when these events happen, they can leave us frustrated, doubting, cynical, and even lost.

Let me stop for a moment because some of you feel as if you are there right now. You are approaching a place in life where you never really thought you would be. Maybe it feels like failure. Maybe it feels like an irreversible setback. Maybe it feels as if everything you thought would be true about your life is slipping away. Maybe it feels as if you are so far off track that there is no way to recover. If this is you, hear this: you aren't the only one. Even this, even your low point, is part of the journey. And how you react right now, how you navigate through this season, and what you choose to do next can define your story. As I am fond of saying to my congregation, your low point is not your last point. And while we would never choose these moments, God can use them to transform and shape us in profound ways.

Here's the truth: "up and to the right" is a myth, pure and simple. Life doesn't work that way. It never has. Setbacks are to be expected. We cannot stop them, we can't wish them away, and it is dangerous to try to avoid them. Low points will be part of your journey, and they are beyond your control. How you react to these moments, though, is entirely up to you, and with God's help, these low points can become your defining moments.

When we last checked in on the Israelites, they were in the middle of the desert—a low point—complaining about the manna they had to eat, frustrated that the promised land seemed far off, growing nostalgic for Egypt, and asking Moses if they could just turn around and go back to where they started. To them, the journey seemed to be leading them nowhere; and even if there really was a land of milk and honey waiting for them at the end, they wondered whether it would really be worth it. As they had at other points along the way, the people questioned their decision to leave. They began to think that the journey is just one slow descent to starvation and death in the desert. Extreme? Maybe. Dramatic? Definitely. But many of us can relate. We set out on a journey to the promised land, only to begin to believe that we are destined to die in the desert.

GOING DOWNHILL FAST

If you have spent any time around a church, you have likely heard about the significance of Mount Sinai. It is an important place, especially in the Old Testament. It appears in the stories of many people, but most famously it plays a starring role in the Israelites' wilderness journey. In fact, if you read the Book of Exodus, just over half the book is about what happens to the Israelites at Mount Sinai. So what is so significant about Sinai? And what in the world does it have to do with us?

The beginning of the Israelites' exodus story is a little like a comedy of errors. They left Egypt with so much anticipation, hope, and promise. They were going to be free, and they were looking forward to a land flowing with milk and honey. They had a powerful God guiding them, with God's servant, Moses, leading them every step of the way. I imagine some of them thought that in no time they would be conquering enemies, establishing new homes, and building their own kingdom in the promised land. So imagine the frustration when, months into their desert journey, they have already experienced several setbacks. It was only days after crossing the Red Sea that they ran out of water and began to think they would die of dehydration. They found the water in the wilderness bitter and undrinkable.

This was just the beginning. Not long after, they thought they were going to starve. They soon grew weary of the food (as we learned in the previous chapter) and began seriously to contemplate going back. Shortly after that, they faced a foreign army that wasn't going to let them pass without a confrontation. Then they had to deal with internal disputes. Add to all this the incessant grumbling and the desire to go back, and what we have is a journey that was not panning out like the luxury ride to the promised land that people had anticipated.

We often give the Israelites a hard time. We look down on them for the way they constantly complained. We like to think that, somehow, we would do it better or be more grateful. We tell ourselves that our own faith would be stronger than theirs. But I have to admit, I have a soft spot for the Israelites. After all, they did what God asked of them. They faithfully followed when God implausibly promised to lead them out of Egypt with a stuttering and inexperienced Moses. They stayed faithful through the plagues, stepped into the water trusting God to part the sea, and followed Moses into a wilderness without a clear plan or knowledge of how long they would be there. And now here they were, months into the journey, and they had run out of water and run into a hostile army. They had lost friends and family to battle. But they still got up every day for another hot march in the desert. And the promised land was nowhere in sight. Sure, things were bad in Egypt. But now that they were in the desert, things didn't seem to be getting better. In fact, the longer they followed God, the worse it seemed to get. What in the world was going on? Had God lost his mojo? Or maybe Moses was the problem. Maybe the Israelites never should have set out on this adventure in the first place. Whatever the cause, and wherever they laid the blame, the situation was clear: things were getting worse.

So I get why the people complained and why they were doubtful. They left Egypt with an expectation of a better life. God neglected to inform them there would be a wilderness period. God had left out the part about thirsting, starving, wandering, and fighting. No one told them that things might get worse before they got better. Like so many of us, the Israelites expected a life following God to be one of blessing. They expected a life that was all "up and to the right." In heading for the peak, they did not understand that they would have to trust God to take them through a number of valleys that would be strange and scary.

Years ago, a pastor friend of mine was appointed to a small, country church in a suburban bedroom community. The church had a long tradition of doing things a certain way. Like so many churches, it was in a long, slow decline. If they kept doing things the same way, it wouldn't be too long before they would have to close the doors. So when this new, young pastor with a family got appointed to their congregation, the members' hopes ran high. The pastor talked about growth, the need for a new vision, and the importance of doing things differently. Because the congregation was eager to save their church, they enthusiastically offered their support for the pastor's plans to change things.

All of this sounded good in theory. But as soon as the promised changes started happening, people quickly changed their minds. They watched beloved traditions end. Longtime ministries no longer received the same attention that they once had. The worship style started to change, and people who had long led certain ministries were asked to step down to make room for others. Things were changing all right, but it didn't seem to be for the better. People became disgruntled. They missed how the church used to be. In frustration and anger, people started to leave the church. In nine months, the church went from an average of one hundred people in worship each Sunday to about sixty.

You can imagine (I certainly can) what the board meetings sounded like during this time. I bet they were questioning this new approach. I bet they doubted that it was really working. I suspect they had some hard questions for the young pastor with a big new vision. They were excited and enthusiastic because they thought that the plan was for the church to *grow*. So if that was the plan, it didn't seem to be going in the right direction. I won't tell you what happened (not yet anyway). But maybe you can guess. For now, I'll just say the attendance for worship never got lower than sixty people. Yes, that first year was hard. It was hard for people to continue to trust that the plan was working. By any visible marker, it seemed just the opposite. And yet while things seemed to be going downhill, they were also setting the stage for something new. This is often how it is with change. Things get harder before they get better.

Sinai is where everything changed for the Israelites. Sinai was their turning point. Sinai can become your turning point as well.

As a more personal example, I have a friend who is a recovering alcoholic. It took him a long time to recognize that he had a drinking problem and finally to stop. But after a lot of mistakes, several interventions, and many prayers, he made the decision to stop drinking. "Life is going to be better without alcohol in it," he told himself.

And it was true. But in the months that followed that decision, it didn't feel that way. My friend found out pretty quickly what a lot of you might know to be true: people often use alcohol just to cope with or avoid other issues in life. Maybe it is dysfunctional relationships, depression, fear, or stress. Alcohol often masks these deeper issues so that we don't have to deal with them. So when my friend stopped drinking, he was expecting life to get better immediately. It didn't. He found himself lonely because many of the friends he had were drinking buddies, and he couldn't spend as much time with them. His years of drinking had taken their toll on his marriage, and he now had to confront and address those problems. During his twelve steps of recovery, he realized the extent to which he had hurt people whom he cared about. Now he had to face up to the damage that he had caused. Finally, he began to realize that he had used drinking to escape some hard realities. With the help of a therapist, he was going to have to "go there" and address some long-repressed "junk" that he was holding onto and that was holding him back.

The truth was that there were days when drinking sounded easier than all this personal work. The first few months of sobriety were not better and easier; they often felt worse and more difficult. Life seemed to be going downhill. He could not yet see that, in reality, the stage was being set for something new to begin.

You've undoubtedly experienced something similar when you were in one of life's valleys. As much as we would love for life to be up and to the right, it rarely works that way. This is especially true when we are in the midst of transition. That is where the Israelites were. The journey was only getting harder. On top of it all, they were no closer to the promised land than when they first started. In fact, they were geographically farther away. If you look on a map, the promised land was up and to the right from Egypt. But that is not what their journey looked like. In fact, if you charted their course, they had been heading south—or, as it appears on a map, straight down!

THE TURNING POINT

Remember the map on your hand? I want you to go back to it. (You can also use a real map, of course; perhaps there is one at the back of your Bible.)

Look at the palm of your left hand. Remember that Egypt is roughly where your thumb is, and the promised land is about where the tip of your pinky finger is. The Israelites expected to go straight into the land that God had promised them, but that is not what happened. Now we already have seen that God was not going to take them by a direct route. We learned that in Exodus. But what we haven't yet learned is where God was leading them first. Before the Israelites got to the promised land, before they could begin taking hold of the new promise, God was actually leading them further away from it. God was leading them the opposite direction.

As you look at your left hand, I want you to look as far

down on your palm as you can, right at the point where your hand meets your wrist. That is where God was leading them first, before the land of milk and honey. Do you know what is significant about this spot on your map? Well, for starters, it is the farthest away that the Israelites could get from the land they were promised. But more important, this was the location of what would become an important place for the Israelites (and many who came after them). It was the location of Mount Sinai, otherwise known as Mount Horeb in the Bible. And something significant happened at Mount Sinai. It was here that the Israelites experienced their turning point.

Let's take a look at an actual map. Most scholars believe that Mount Sinai sits at the very bottom of what is known as the Sinai Peninsula. It was here that God was leading the Israelites. Exodus tells us that they reached this spot on the map three months into their journey: "On exactly the third-month anniversary of the Israelites' leaving the land of Egypt, they came into the Sinai desert. They traveled from Rephidim, came into the Sinai desert, and set up camp there. Israel camped there in front of the mountain" (Exodus 19:1-2).

Three months into the trip, this is the situation. This journey to the promised land should have taken a few weeks, maybe a month, tops. But instead, the Israelites geographically were farther away from their destination than when they started. They also were further away in a figurative sense. That is why I am making such a big deal about the map. I want you to see that, in a literal sense, the people were traveling away from the goal. But the more important point is that, spiritually and emotionally, it felt like they were going in completely the wrong direction. The Israelites left Egypt intending to change, to grow, to follow God, and to arrive somewhere better. But that is not what was happening. Life felt worse, the journey felt hopeless, and they were nowhere near their intended destination.

Mount Sinai is a real place. You can visit it. But even if you have never been to Egypt, you still know Sinai. It represents a place where we have all been. It was not only the lowest geographical point they would reach on their journey but also their figurative low point, their rock bottom. It was where their hope dried up and their faith in God faltered. It was the point of their greatest temptation and the place where the people finally gave up on trusting God. We know what this feels like. We have all been to Sinai.

But you know what? Sinai would also become the Israelites' defining moment. From this point on, the journey would look different, feel different, and follow a different trajectory. God was going to do something with them and for them at Sinai that would prepare them to become the people God wanted them to be. Sinai is where everything changed for the Israelites. Sinai was their turning point. I want to show you how Sinai can become your turning point as well.

Let me come back to the energetic pastor who tried to make changes for a congregation that seemed to be stuck in the wilderness. When their Sunday worship attendance declined from one hundred to sixty people, it looked like death, like failure. They seemed to be headed down and to the left instead of up and to the right. But God was doing something even in that decline. God was working when most people couldn't see it. God loves comebacks and turnaround stories. God loves to show God's power precisely at the point when our own power runs out. That way, we know that credit for the success should be given to God and not to us. That way, we know that God is present and active.

When the attendance shrank to sixty people, that church was already undergoing major change. A small remnant of people couldn't handle it, but those sixty stuck with it and would eventually be glad they did. That board hung in there, and it was a good thing. The church started to reach new people, started to grow, and started to make a noticeable impact. The changes first led to precipitous decline, but that was a head fake. It was merely clearing the way for something new. There needed to be some pruning in order to make room for new growth. Then the changes started bearing fruit.

I don't believe that God causes hardship, pain, and suffering just to teach us a lesson.

Over the next several decades, that church grew explosively. It would end up reaching thousands of people to become one of the largest United Methodist congregations in the country. Its work affected hundreds of young pastors, and that lead pastor would go on to mentor and influence the work of a new generation of leaders, including me. The low point wasn't the last point. It didn't last. In fact, that low point, when the people of that congregation were in the midst of the fear and uncertainty of the wilderness, ended up being their Sinai. It would become their mountaintop and their defining moment.

It can be the same way for you. During your journey through significant change and transition, life may very well get worse before it gets better. The lesson of the Israelites gives us something of a road map. It normalizes those times in our life when we seem to be taking one step forward and two steps back, moving further away from where we thought we were heading. If you feel that's how things are going for you right now, it is a good sign that you are in a Sinai moment. It feels like a low point. But what we will see is that God can do some of God's most important work when we are feeling at our lowest. Maybe it is because our defenses are down or our pride is no longer in the way. Maybe it is because in our low points we finally give up the illusion that we can do it ourselves. Maybe our low points humble and soften our hearts enough for God to shape and remold them.

STRENGTH FROM WEAKNESS

In the New Testament, the apostle Paul wrote about his own personal struggles. He never tells us exactly what the challenge was, but he reflects on its significance in his life:

Therefore, in order to keep me from becoming conceited, I was given a thorn in my flesh, a messenger of Satan, to torment me. Three times I pleaded with the Lord to take it away from me. But he said to me, "My grace is sufficient for you, for my power is made perfect in weakness." Therefore I will boast all the more gladly about my weaknesses, so that Christ's power may rest on me. That is why, for Christ's sake, I delight in weaknesses, in insults, in hardships, in persecutions, in difficulties. For when I am weak, then I am strong.

(2 Corinthians 12:7b-10 NIV)

Paul begins by admitting that he was given a significant personal challenge, a "thorn in the flesh." It was obviously something that caused him great hardship because he attributes it to a "messenger of Satan," something that tormented him. But over time this "thorn" actually became the grounds by which God began to work in Paul's life. He believed the challenge humbled him in a way that made him rely less on self and more on God. He then makes one of the most counterintuitive claims in the Bible. He says that now he sees seasons of weakness as something to actually delight in. Why? Because when he is weak, he is strong!

I think what Paul means is that God has enough power, enough might, and enough creativity that God can actually take our weaknesses and turn them into strengths. God can take seasons of personal struggle and use them to shape us in positive ways. God can take our seasons of weakness and from those experiences give us a mission, passion, or calling that we may never have found without that struggle. God actually shows up even more in our times of weakness as if to say to us, "See, I am not leaving you alone." At the same time, it is as if God is saying to the world, "See I can even work miracles at the absolute lowest points in people's lives." It is almost proof that God is God, that God is present, and that God is powerful.

All of this is meant to be a solace to us, even an encouragement. Our low points, our own seasons of weakness, can actually set the stage for God to do something significant in and through us. It turned out that God would shape Israel at Sinai in ways that would define the people up into the present time. Sinai is remembered, even today, as a defining moment for the people of Israel. Sinai is now remembered, not as a low point, but as a mountaintop experience. It was on the mountaintop that they received the law, and it was through trying to live by the law over the ensuing centuries that they came to understand that God had chosen them as the people through whom the wider world would come to know God. But it didn't seem that way for the people going through it.

> *The problem with "everything happens for a reason" is that it leads to human indifference.*

Similarly, your life is going to hit seasons—especially as you navigate change—when you feel like you are heading downhill fast. This is the dip. Don't lose hope. Don't give up. Don't throw in the towel. This is your Sinai. It could become your mountaintop experience and, by God's grace, your defining moment.

Your life is not always going to be up and to the right. That chart is a myth. If you want a better one, try this. Have you ever seen a graph showing the performance of the stock market over the past century? In 1928, the year before the Great Crash, the Dow Jones Industrial Average was less than 300. At the end of 2000, it was almost 11,000. In 2018, it peaked at nearly 27,000. That's an amazing trajectory. But the progress was anything but steady. If you look at the market's performance as a graph, it's full of peaks and valleys. Even within the course of one day there can be dramatic swings up or down. Our journey to the promised land is much more likely to resemble the performance of the stock market than a simple graph that steadily moves up and to the right. There will be high points and low points, boom times and depressions. That doesn't mean we won't reach a satisfying end to our journey. But if we allow ourselves to think that the low point is the last point, we can lose our way and miss the richness of life that God wants us to enjoy.

ALWAYS FOR GOOD

But before I get to the kinds of lessons that God can teach us in the low points in our life (in chapter 7), there is an important, nuanced point that I want to make. I don't believe that God causes hardship, pain, and suffering just to teach us a lesson. Scripture seems to indicate that, at times, God may intentionally have us go through some kind of challenge in order to teach, discipline, or shape us. I often meet people who believe everything that happens in our life happens because of God, according to some divine plan. I know this is a popular thing for some of us to believe because, quite honestly, it is easier during times of hardship to believe that "everything happens for a reason."

That way of thinking has some truth to it and some benefits. Recently, I got stuck in the slow line at the grocery store. Does that ever happen to you? Like many of you, I am impatient. I started mumbling some not-very-nice things under my breath. As I was standing there, the person in front of me was arguing about the cost of a certain item, and the cashier pulled the little cord to start the infamous blinking light to summon the manager. I knew this situation could take a while to resolve, which meant that I would be standing there waiting. As I started to get angry, I told myself, "Matt, this happened for a reason. God obviously needed you to slow down, practice patience, pay attention to the small things around you, or just learn to be present in the moment." I began to tell myself that there was some lesson to be learned here, some purpose for which I had to suffer this inconvenience. And you know what? It worked. I grew a bit less frustrated, and suddenly I focused much less on waiting and much more on finding that reason why I was waiting. The whole encounter actually made me a better person (even if I forgot the lesson the next time I had to wait in a line unexpectedly).

In some situations like this, I get it. "Everything happens for a reason" is a nice way to attempt to make sense of life. It is a way of redirecting our anger and frustration, reminding ourselves to trust in God, and remembering that God can ultimately do something good even amidst a bad situation. It can work, and it does. And that is why a lot of us like it.

But, sometimes, in our effort to be helpful, we apply this idea to ever more serious situations. The frustrating wait at the grocery store is one thing. But pretty soon we use the same reasoning to explain the fender bender in the parking lot, the friend who hurts our feelings, or the boss who treats us unfairly. Pretty soon the life situations get more serious—divorce, the loss of a job, suicide, cancer, rape, tragic death, hurricanes, genocide, and the list goes on. Somewhere in that spectrum, the easy answer that helped me get through the grocery line breaks down. It doesn't work. It becomes a problem to think that God somehow ordains each of these to happen as part of a larger "plan."

There are two big problems with this line of thinking. First, it makes God responsible for everything that happens in our life and in the world. Consider just some of the things that were on my prayer list at the time of writing this chapter.

I was praying for a coworker of mine who was murdered in late 2018 in a random act of violence. She left behind four adult children and a number of grandchildren. She was a teacher, a lover of children, and a compassionate friend to many.

I was praying for the country of Mozambique, where tens of thousands of people live every day without safe water and basic medical care. The life expectancy in that country is fifty-eight years, compared to seventy-nine years in the United States. Each year our church gives away 100 percent of our Christmas Eve offering in order to dig wells for clean water in Mozambique.

I was praying for a good friend of mine who is going through a painful divorce and trying to work out how to best co-parent two young children.

I was praying for a parishioner of mine who just found out that her daughter is struggling with depression and has twice attempted suicide.

I could go on.

If everything happens for a reason, then it means that somehow God caused these things to happen. It would mean there is some reason for the murder of my friend and staff person. It would mean that the extreme poverty and injustice in the world are part of God's plan. It would mean that the God who desires a life of purpose and fulfillment for each of God's children planned for a young woman to believe her life wasn't worth living. If you believe that, then you have to contend with a God who doesn't seem anything like the God scripture describes when it says things like: "The LORD is compassionate and merciful, very patient, and full of faithful love" (Psalm 103:8).

Thinking that everything happens for a reason is problematic because it makes God responsible for every horrific tragedy in our world.

The second problem with "everything happens for a reason" is that it leads to human indifference. If there is a master plan, and everything happens according to that plan, then it doesn't leave much room for choice, personal responsibility, or action. Instead, it can lead to inaction in the face of injustice, hardship, hurt, or tragedy. After all, if these were all part of God's plan, who are we to interfere, right? But the Bible makes it clear that we have real choices and a responsibility to follow God's hopes and teachings.

I don't believe that everything happens for a reason or that God causes all of our hardships. What I do believe, and what I think scripture teaches us, is that God does not cause our pain but is present in our pain. God can work in the rubble of our broken lives to bring about good for us. There is no life situation so bad that God cannot bring about some kind of good from it. This is what Paul means when he writes:

> In the same way, the Spirit comes to help our weakness. We don't know what we should pray, but the Spirit himself pleads our case with unexpressed groans. The one who searches hearts knows how the Spirit thinks, because he pleads for the saints, consistent with God's will. We know that God works all things together for good for the ones who love God, for those who are called according to his purpose. (Romans 8:26-28)

God has a broad plan for us, a plan to bring us wholeness, not harm, to give us life abundant, and to use us as part of God's eternal purposes. God is not absent in our life, and God can weave the broken strands of our life back together. God is always at work, especially in our broken moments and lowest points, to teach us, mold us, re-create us, and save us. In this sense, God will use low points to change us.

It is important that we understand this because in the next chapter I want to talk about how God can use your low points to actually benefit you. But as we go there, remember that while God doesn't cause these moments, God can transform every low point into our Sinai, our mountaintop experience.

Chapter 7

THE TURNAROUND

—⁓—

I used to be embarrassed about failures, scared to show weakness, and silent about my low moments in ministry. I did this from a false belief that it was my strengths that others wanted to see. I did it because I believed that, if people saw my struggles, they would think less of me. I was wrong. Our strengths are of little interest to others. It is our weaknesses that make us interesting and our struggles that give our life texture and depth. Our strengths rarely teach us as much as our weaknesses do. Transparency about our strengths can easily come off as bragging, but transparency about our weaknesses can immediately make space for others to open up. Nothing is quite as powerful and transformative for others as operating out of your God-transformed weaknesses. That is why the lessons we learn in our low points can define us, reshape us, and help us discover our authentic purpose and passion.

The stories of the Israelites at Mount Sinai are some of the most memorable and impactful of any in the wilderness. More than half of the Book of Exodus is about what God did with and for the people at Sinai. The older I get, the more I begin to think that the most transformative parts of my story come from my low points and weaknesses. When I speak to other pastors, they want to hear about my struggles in ministry. When I talk to other married couples, they want to know how we navigated through our rough seasons. When I talk to fellow leaders, we want to talk about those seasons of failure, what we learned, and how we emerged from them. I am convinced that God uses our low points to turn us around, re-form us, teach us, and give us a clearer purpose and vision.

In the preceding chapter, we talked about the descent, the dip, the journey that seemed to take the Israelites farther away from where they thought they were headed. But at Sinai all of that changed. They hit the geographical low point, and from there the journey literally turned around. Spiritually speaking, Sinai was a turnaround moment as well. Several things happened at Sinai that began to point the people back up toward the purposes that God had for them. Similarly, in our lives something can happen in our low points to turn our life around and to point us toward the new reality that God has in store for us. If we are open to the lessons to be learned in low points, they can shape us for the rest of our lives.

LESSONS FROM THE LOW POINTS

I want you to bring to mind a low point in your life. Maybe it is *the* low point—the day a marriage fell apart, the moment you received a scary diagnosis, the time you went to work only to find out your job was no more, or the second you learned that you lost someone you love. Maybe your rock bottom was when you realized you needed help and that you couldn't do life alone. Maybe your low point felt like a pit of depression, a wave of regret, a surge of shame, or a flood of despair. Whenever it was, whatever the circumstances, I want you to bring it to mind.

Our culture may value self-sufficiency, but it is not a value of God's. God uses the wilderness to teach us that we need God and that we aren't meant to do it alone.

If you are going through your low point right now, you are going to have to hold tight and trust me on this one. But for those of you who can remember a low point from the past, I want you to consider something. Did your low point change you? Did it lead to anything good in your life? Are you able to look back on it now and see that something significant happened to you and for you in that moment? Now, I am not suggesting that this bad thing was actually a good thing or that you would want to go back or choose it all over again. Please don't misunderstand me. All I am pointing out is that, in retrospect, we can usually see the way that God moved in our life, even in some of our darkest moments. Those moments, whether we wish it or not, change us, teach us, shape us, and make us the people we are today. The same would ultimately be true of the Israelites. Sinai became an important milestone on their journey to becoming a new people prepared for a new land. So let's look at what happens at Sinai and how our low points can change and shape us.

1. Low points force us to accept help.

During my first year of pastoring The Gathering, I preached fifty-one weeks out of fifty-two. I didn't do this because there was no one else. In fact, several retired pastors who were connected to the congregation, as well as a few very capable laypeople, could have preached in my stead. I did it because I thought I needed to. I thought that, if I wasn't there, then the service would not be as good; and if the service wasn't as good, people would stop coming. It is embarrassing now to write this, but it is true. I thought that even one bad Sunday could throw everything out of whack. So I never took a weekend off.

On top of that, I worked an average of sixty to seventy hours a week. I met everyone who wanted to meet with me, followed up with every new visitor myself, made the coffee, shoveled the sidewalks, led several small groups, and regularly checked (and returned) emails late into the night. If there was a meeting, I thought I had to be there. If there was a church event, I believed that I had to attend. If someone needed me, I felt obligated to bend and twist my schedule to accommodate the request. In short, I did almost everything. I couldn't say no to anyone because I was afraid of disappointing them. Most of all, I thought that the success of the church would rise and fall based on my willingness to work hard. I thought I was being faithful. I thought I was being sacrificial. I believed that I was doing what needed to be done for a new ministry to take off. In reality, I was being stupid. More than that, I was misguided and scared.

falsely believed that leadership meant everything for everybody. Underneath that was fear—fear that perhaps I wasn't up to the task, fear of failing, fear of disappointing, and maybe even fear of inadequacy. I thought that the answer to each of these fears was to work harder, never to say no, and to push through when I was tired. This overwork contributed to the impending crisis in my personal life that I experienced that year.

Overworking never made me feel like I had gotten ahead; it only led me deeper and deeper into a hole that I could never escape, no matter how many extra hours I put in. Something had to change. While I couldn't quite admit it out loud, I knew the pace I was keeping was not sustainable. I knew that I wasn't going to make it. I knew that my habits weren't healthy or faithful to my calling. The only problem is, I didn't know what to do about it. So I kept going until I simply couldn't do it anymore. On the verge of burnout, I was ready to quit. And finally I did something that was so simple and made so much sense. I asked for help.

As the Israelites were arriving at Sinai, Moses received a visit from his father-in-law, Jethro. As a priest and fellow leader, Jethro knew the difficulties of being in charge. After an evening of swapping stories and catching up, Moses woke up the next day to resume his work of leading the people, and Jethro had a chance to observe him. What happened next is a story that every leader should read at least once a year:

> The next day Moses sat as a judge for the people, while the people stood around Moses from morning until evening. When Moses's father-in-law saw all that he was doing for the people, he said, "What's this that you are doing for the people? Why do you sit alone, while all the people are standing around you from morning until evening?" . . . "What you are doing isn't good. You will end up totally wearing yourself out, both you and these people who are with you. The work is too difficult for you. You can't do it alone. Now listen to me and let me give you some advice. And may God be with you! . . . But you should also look among all the people for capable persons who respect God. They should be trustworthy and not corrupt. Set these persons over the people as officers of groups of thousands, hundreds, fifties, and tens. . . . This will be much easier for you, and they will share your load. If you do this and God directs you, then you will be able to endure."
>
> (Exodus 18:13-14, 17-19a, 21, 22b)

You don't need to be a priest, a pastor, or a leader to understand this. Here was Moses, killing himself day in and day out serving, listening, judging, and arbitrating conflict. Every day, Moses felt the burden of the leadership that rested squarely on his shoulders. Every day, he acted as if it were all up to him. When he was on the verge of burnout, after multiple frustrating encounters with the people, Jethro gave him some simple advice: ask for help.

I wish that it didn't take a low point for us to listen

to Jethro's advice, but often it does. We live in a culture that values independence. Doing it ourselves is a virtue, and progressively becoming less dependent on the people around us is often portrayed in our society as maturity. "Good" leaders know what they are doing and don't need advice. "Good" marriages don't need counseling or therapy. "Good" parents have it together and don't need to read books, take a class, or seek help. Asking for help is often seen as a weakness. We are slow to admit that maybe we can't do it ourselves. This infatuation with independence hurts us when we move through transition, pursue change, or follow a new call in our life.

Our culture may value self-sufficiency, but it is not a value of God's. In fact, God uses the wilderness to teach us that we are dependent, that we need God and others, and that we aren't meant to do it alone. The problem is that we often will not truly hear that message until we hit the proverbial brick wall. It seems to take a low point for us to realize that we can't do it alone (and that we don't have to). In these moments we realize that God is ready to help us and that we need the people whom God puts around us. It often takes our failure before we realize that depending on others around us is not only a necessity but also a blessing. Only when he was on the verge of burnout and failure was Moses able to listen to his father-in-law's advice and start sharing his burden with the people God placed around him.

We can learn this lesson every time we find our own efforts falling short—in managing our mental health, in parenting, in a professional endeavor, in beating an addiction or habit, in forging a healthy marriage, or in learning a new skill. In each of these cases it often takes fatigue, burnout, or failure before we will ask for help. As painful as they can be, low points teach us that we can't do life alone and that we are meant to. God surrounds us in our low points, reminds us that there is help all around us. It is a painful but powerful lesson that we need to learn if we are going to continue to journey toward a new reality in our life.

2. Low points make us teachable.

Mount Sinai is probably best known as the place where God gave the law to Moses and the Israelites. In fact, if you try reading the Book of Exodus, right after chapter 20 the story runs a little dry. For the twelve chapters that follow, all we read is verse after verse of instructions and laws for the people. But chapters 19 and 20 tell the story of Sinai. God summoned Moses up onto the mountain, came to him in a dense cloud, and spoke to him in thunder. God said that the Israelites are to be consecrated as a holy people; in other words, God was not just rescuing them from Egypt but giving them a mission. And then God gave Moses the Ten Commandments.

It can be easy to skip right over the laws that were given at Sinai, but I want us to think a little bit about the connection between Israel's low point and God's instructions. God easily could have given them the laws right when they left Egypt. God could have written each family their own little stone tablet copy of the laws to have with them as soon as they left Egypt. But God didn't do that. God led the people into the wilderness without any real instructions. God led them down the Sinai Peninsula, and in frustration and doubt they questioned what God was doing. It was only when they reached the mountain that God decided to give them the law. We often think that the word *law* has negative connotations. We think of dry lists of commandments or a God devoid of grace and forgiveness. We often imagine the law to be somehow opposite of mercy and love. But this is not the case.

> *Learning to become new people is hard. Being transformed doesn't always feel good. Allowing God to instruct, discipline, and shape you isn't easy.*

When God gave Israel the law, he was teaching them a new way to live. Part of their preparation for the promised land was that they had to let go of old ways of thinking and being, strategies that might have worked in Egypt but would have no place in the promised land. In the wilderness, they had to learn new patterns and ways of living. These new patterns would shape them as God's people, would set them apart from other nations, and would prepare them for the change of life that was coming. God had to teach them how to be new people so they could occupy a new land and fulfill a new call.

The same is true for us. Before we can experience change in our lives "out there," we often have to undergo a change inside our own hearts and minds. We have to let go of old ways of thinking and being so that God can teach us new patterns of living that are consistent with the new direction of our life.

But what does any of this have to do with low points? Well, I have come to see that while God can teach me pretty much anytime in my life, there are certain lessons and instructions I can receive only through seasons of struggle and challenge. There is something about hitting rock bottom that opens me up to new directions for my life. It is only when my old way of life stops working that I am open to new lessons that I had previously ignored or avoided.

I have a friend who went through a painful divorce several years ago. It was not a separation of his own choosing. In this particular case, he found out his wife was involved in another relationship. After a confrontation, it became clear that the marriage wasn't going to be saved. She wanted to be out, and despite my friend's desire to the contrary, the marriage ended in divorce. For my friend, it was a season of low points. He felt like a failure, he was grieving for the loss of this marriage, and he felt like he was suddenly thrust into a wilderness of uncertainty that he didn't choose. Hope was in short supply, and it was hard to see a way forward.

But over time, things began to change. After the initial shock of loss he decided to visit a counselor and start investing new energy in his spiritual life. After several hard months, he began to see light in what previously was only a dark tunnel. As much as he didn't want a divorce, he began to see that this moment forced him to look at aspects of his life and reconsider how he was living. I don't believe God "caused" the divorce, but God used the divorce to teach my friend new ways to live. His self-awareness, ability to connect with others, and faith in God all changed and grew dramatically through this season. In hindsight, he sees that, as painful as the low point was, it afforded him the opportunity to learn important lessons that he never would have learned otherwise. As painful as it was, God also used it to change him for the better.

It is often that way with low points. Remember, I don't think God causes every tragedy, challenge, or obstacle in your life *just* to teach you some lesson. That would be a cruel God. But God can use our wilderness times and our low points to teach us new ways of living. Maybe it is our desperation, humility, or our fragility, but there is something about suffering that opens us up to God in a new and unique way. Sinai was not the only place where God would instruct Israel, but there were lessons they learned here that they perhaps couldn't learn anywhere else.

3. Low points give us new purpose.

When God gave Moses the law for the Israelites, it was about more than simply instructing them on a new way to live. God was preparing them for their mission. To remember their mission, you have to go all the way back to Abraham, to the very first covenant God made with Abraham. We read it earlier, but let me remind you of it here: "The LORD said to Abram, 'Leave your land, your family, and your father's household for the land that I will show you. I will make of you a great nation and will bless you. I will make your name respected, and you will be a blessing' " (Genesis 12:1-2).

God didn't just choose to free Israel, lead them through the desert, and give them a promised land for themselves. God had a much greater purpose in mind. Israel was blessed and chosen by God in order for God to use them to bless others. They were blessed to be a blessing. We see this theme crop up over and over again in scripture. God didn't just make this promise to Abraham but confirmed it to Isaac and eventually to Jacob (whom God renamed later as Israel). God told Jacob: "I am the LORD, the God of your father Abraham and the God of Isaac. I will give you and your descendants the land on which you are lying. Your descendants will become like the dust of the earth; you will spread out to the west, east, north, and south. Every family of earth will be blessed because of you and your descendants" (Genesis 28:13b-14).

Much later, as God is bringing the Israelites from exile in Babylon back to the promised land, the prophet Isaiah remembers this larger mission:

> [God] said: It is not enough, since you are my
>   servant,
>   to raise up the tribes of Jacob
>   and to bring back the survivors of Israel.
>   Hence, I will also appoint you as light to the
>   nations
>   so that my salvation may reach to the end of
>   the earth. (Isaiah 49:6)

Ultimately, the first Christians saw Jesus as a fulfillment of this promise to use the chosen people of Israel to be salvation, a light and blessing, to all people. Simeon, a Temple prophet at the time of Jesus's birth, proclaimed the fulfillment of this ancient promise as soon as he laid eyes on the infant Jesus, proclaiming:

> Now, master, let your servant go in peace
>   according to your word,
>   because my eyes have seen your salvation.
> You prepared this salvation in the presence of
>   all peoples.
> It's a light for revelation to the Gentiles
>   and a glory for your people Israel.
>   (Luke 2:29-32)

I could keep going, but you get the point. God had a much larger purpose for Israel than simply releasing them from Egypt, leading them through the desert, and setting them up in a new land. God was doing all this so that God could use them to be a witness to the world, a light to all nations, and a blessing to all people. God was not leading the Israelites through all this transformation and transition just for them. God had a much bigger mission in mind for them.

At Sinai, as God gave the people the law, God wasn't trying to get them to follow some set of arbitrary rules. God was giving them a new way to live as a way to prepare them to be light to all people. God had to transform them so that God could use them to transform others.

But learning to become new people is hard. Being

transformed doesn't always feel good. As the Israelites learned, allowing God to instruct, discipline, and shape you isn't easy. It is one thing to say that we want God to change us. It is another thing to actually allow God to do it. In many ways, Mount Sinai was the place where God began to instruct the people and change their lives so that they could be the light-bearers and world-blessers that God intended them to be. But in order to do that, they had to spend time at that low point of Sinai.

God can use our low points in very much the same way. When we go through trials in our life, God doesn't just use those times to shape and teach us. God can often use those moments to give us a mission or prepare us to be used in the lives of others. Often, our low points become the arena in which we discover our mission and how our life could be used to influence, serve, and bless others. In this way, God redeems our struggles by preparing us to serve others out of those very places of weakness.

I have a good friend whom I met when he was drinking—a lot. He was an alcoholic. I could see it. The people who loved him could see it. The only problem was that he couldn't see it. When he finally decided it was time to change and went to Alcoholics Anonymous, he was in for a shock. He thought the main problem was the drinking, and the solution would be to change this one little area of his life. What he learned is that, in order to become a new person, a person who didn't drink, he was going to have to learn an entirely new way to live. But walking through that process and doing the hard work necessary to get to a new place helped him also discover something else: a purpose. He realized that the road he walked was so lonely and so difficult, that he now felt called by God to help others who were just beginning the same journey. Today he leads AA meetings, mentors and sponsors others in recovery, and meets with countless people who are contemplating this change in their own life.

His low point actually gave him a new purpose for his life, and your low points can do the same for you.

4. Low points shatter our idols.

Perhaps the most famous story from the Israelites' time at Sinai is the story of the golden calf. Upon arriving at the mountain, God instructed Moses to leave the people at the base of the mountain and then climb up to meet God. On the mountain, God spoke to Moses, giving him the law. This was not a quick trip up the hill. The Bible says that Moses made several trips up Mount Sinai. On at least one occasion, he was there for forty days and forty nights. During this time, the Israelites finally hit their breaking point. They had listened to God, they had followed God, and now they were waiting for God. Finally, they simply couldn't do it anymore. Instead of reaching the promised land, they were hundreds of miles south of their goal, at the base of a mountain in the wilderness. Moses had asked them to wait just a little longer while he went up to get revised direction from God. But where was he? Why had he been up there for so long? The Israelites were frustrated, out of faith, and no longer willing to wait. At the base of Sinai, they finally did the very thing

God had asked them—begged them—never to do. They gave up on God.

If you recall the story, the Israelites left Egypt with more than their lives and freedom. The Egyptians had given them lots of gold. After all, they had already suffered from ten horrible plagues; they didn't want any more devastation on their land. So when the Israelites asked them for gold, the Egyptians gave. In a way the Israelites had not expected, God had given them a great treasure that they could use to build new lives in the promised land. But instead, they melted the gold and fashioned it into a statue of a golden calf and began to worship this idol. They were done waiting on God, and they were impatient with Moses, who had been up on the mountain for a long time. It was time to move on. They would make a god of their own. Moses's own brother, Aaron, helped make the idol.

God saw what was happening down at the bottom of Sinai and alerted Moses. He told him that he had better get down the mountain, for the people had made a grave mistake. Moses rushed down, and this was the scene:

> When he got near the camp and saw the bull calf and the dancing, Moses was furious. He hurled the tablets down and shattered them in pieces at the foot of the mountain. He took the calf that they had made and burned it in a fire. Then he ground it down to crushed powder, scattered it on the water, and made the Israelites drink it. Moses said to Aaron, "What did these people do to you that you led them to commit such a terrible sin?" (Exodus 32:19-21)

It wasn't a pretty picture. Moses came down and couldn't believe what he saw. He couldn't believe that the people had put their trust in an inanimate golden statue, somehow believing that this "thing" could do for them what God had promised to do. The scene would be comical if it weren't so serious. In anger, Moses threw down the tablets, destroyed the golden calf, ground it up, and made the Israelites drink it. He called them out for the disloyalty, unfaithfulness, and rebellions that they just demonstrated. It was not a good day. In fact, this day was their low point, the day they gave up on God and started putting their faith in idols. It wasn't be the first time humans made this mistake, and it wouldn't be the last.

Even good things can be idols when
we put them ahead of God.

It is easy to read this story and snicker at the foolishness of the Israelites. After all, who would worship and put their trust in a golden calf? It is silly. A golden calf isn't alive, a golden calf isn't powerful, and a golden calf can't do anything for us when we are in trouble. We may laugh, but before we do, we may want to stop and think. For we all have idols, every one of us. Maybe we don't put our trust in a golden calf, but we place our hope and trust in equally foolish things. What happened to the Israelites at Sinai is that they discovered that their idols were worthless;

the statue that they put their trust in was ineffective to help them. The same thing happens when we hit our own low points. Our idols are revealed for what they are: ineffective to help us.

When it comes to my own life and ministry, I can look back and identify several seasons when I felt like I had reached a low point. My professional and personal rock bottom came about a year into starting The Gathering. The ironic thing is that the church thrived after its launch in the fall of 2006, months after that first practice worship service. People were coming, the energy was good, and commitment was high. But while the church going so well, I was not doing well at all. I was caught in a downward spiral fueled by stress, overwork, emotional immaturity, and inability to deal with pressure. I was uncertain about how to respond to criticism and ineffective in balancing the demands of home and work. I was struggling badly, and yet I didn't want to tell anyone. I didn't want it to appear as if I couldn't do the job. I felt the pressure to be invincible, to show no weakness, and to carry the load myself. It was incredibly foolish and immature. Pretty soon, I was failing as a father, a husband, and a pastor. Though I was never formally diagnosed, in retrospect, I am convinced I was also depressed. All this finally led to an internal crisis that left me calling my supervisors in The United Methodist Church and preparing to resign from the ministry. I felt like a complete failure. It was, and continues to be, one of the most painful seasons of my life. It was my Mount Sinai.

Now, you may be wondering what happened. Well, I am

here, twelve years later, still pastoring The Gathering and writing about it. So you can deduce that there was a positive resolution. While there is much I can say about that painful season (and much that I will share in the pages to come), one significant transformation that happened for me in that low point is that my idols were revealed. I didn't worship a golden calf, but I misplaced the source of my hope and trust. Somewhere along the line, I had stopped trusting and believing God. And that was basically what the Israelites did when they made a golden idol. I stopped remembering that this was God's call and God's ministry, not my own. I began to forget that it was God's Spirit who was leading the way and God's power that was fueling the work. Somewhere along the line, I started thinking that the world depended on me, my capabilities, and my work ethic. I started believing that I was the source of the successes and failures, that my work was the nonnegotiable essential, and that I was responsible for carrying the load of stress and pressure that the church produced. In short, I began to place my trust in my own ability to figure it out and my own capacity to work hard. It was a near-fatal mistake, and it was just as foolish in its own way as worshipping a golden calf.

In some ways, the pain of my low point was also my salvation. The pain came from finally hitting a brick wall and realizing that I wasn't strong enough, smart enough, mature enough, or good enough to lead this church and be the husband and father I wanted to be. My own efforts to do it alone had failed miserably, and I found myself needy, hurting, and dependent. My idol had been shattered. That was the painful part. The transformative part is that only in the wake of that failure did I realize how much I needed God and how far I had strayed from trusting God. My low point also became a transformational moment of turning back toward the God I had wandered from.

God is not done with you yet. There is something yet ahead, a new land, a new reality, and a new beginning.

If you can remember your low point, chances are you can also see a similar pattern. Chances are that your low point also helped you see that you were placing your trust and your hope in something or someone other than God. Some of us place our hope in achievements, successes, or recognition. For others, we place our hope in material possessions, money, or resources. Some of us place too much hope in people such as bosses, coworkers, friends, and even family. For yet others of us, we place our hope in our own abilities. We expect so many of these things to provide us direction, security, ability to overcome challenges, or comfort in trying times. But the problem is that, in reality, all of these things are idols. That is not to say they are *bad*. Idols are not all bad. What I mean is that even good things can be idols when we put them ahead of God. Work, friends, hobbies, having fun, and enjoying life are not bad things. But when they take priority over God in our life, and when we expect them to provide only the things God can provide, they become idols.

The problem with idols, though, is that they are temporary, they are changing and shifting, and at some point, they will fail us. There will come moments in life that family can't fix or money can't solve. There are times when all the notoriety or achievements in the world will not be able to help us resolve a difficult situation we are going through. In those moments when our idols are revealed as wanting, we are left exposed. In those moments, we have a decision to make. We can choose cynicism, anger, bitterness, or despair. We can choose to stay in the pit. Or we can choose to turn toward the one source of hope and trust that isn't temporary and is capable of seeing us through. Our low points can be times of renewed trust in God and a reorienting of our hope back to the one who is worthy of it. Low points can be painful and yet important reminders that too much of our hope and trust is being put in the wrong places.

5. Low points show us our strength and creativity.

Pain and tragedy force us to imagine a life we otherwise would not have to imagine. Think about it. How many times, upon seeing tragedy in the life of another person, have you said to yourself, "I can't imagine what that would be like"? And you are right: you can't imagine what it is like—until something like that happens to you. When you hit a low point, suddenly you have to process it, and you have to pull from a deep well of reserve creativity, energy, and endurance to begin to imagine a life that heretofore you never could have imagined. For that reason, low points can show us the immense strength that we have (and that perhaps we never knew we had before that moment).

The Israelites were not the only famous biblical characters to spend time on Mount Sinai. Hundreds of years after the golden calf debacle, the prophet Elijah fled to Mount Sinai out of fear. Answering God's call, he had just challenged (and dramatically defeated) the false gods of king Ahab and Jezebel. He had his own mountaintop experience, an amazing high point. Then Jezebel vowed to kill him and sent a messenger to tell him so. The Book of 1 Kings tells us what happened next:

> Elijah was afraid and ran for his life. When he came to Beersheba in Judah, he left his servant there, while he himself went a day's journey into the wilderness. He came to a broom bush, sat down under it and prayed that he might die. "I have had enough, LORD," he said. "Take my life; I am no better than my ancestors." Then he lay down under the bush and fell asleep. All at once an angel touched him and said, "Get up and eat." . . . So he got up and ate and drank. Strengthened by that food, he traveled forty days and forty nights until he reached Horeb, the mountain of God.
>
> (1 Kings 19:3-5, 8 NIV)

A few things strike me about this story. By most accounts, it sounds as if Elijah might suffer from what we call depression and what the biblical writers often called despair. He was tired, worn out, alone, and feeling hopeless.

He ran out of fear of what might happen to him at the hands of Jezebel. And the place he ended up was the mountain, the same place his ancestors had been hundreds of years ago. He was at his wits' end. His strength had finally given out, and so he seemed to give in to fear, disillusionment, and dejection. He lay down on the mountain and gave up. He told God that he was done. He wanted to die. Elijah went from the highest high to rock bottom.

But then something happened. In that rock-bottom moment, an angel touched him. Speaking words of encouragement, the angel told Elijah to get up, to eat, and to drink. He did, and in an almost supernatural way found strength that just moments before had eluded him. That strength propelled him to the nearby Mount Horeb (most scholars believe this was just another name for Mount Sinai). It was there that he met God in a new, creative way and discovered a passion that would help him carry out the rest of his prophetic ministry. This is what happened at the mountain:

> There he went into a cave and spent the night. The Lord's word came to him and said, "Why are you here, Elijah?" Elijah replied, "I've been very passionate for the Lord God of heavenly forces because the Israelites have abandoned your covenant. They have torn down your altars, and they have murdered your prophets with the sword. I'm the only one left, and now they want to take my life too!" The Lord said, "Go out and stand at the mountain before the Lord. The Lord is passing by." A very strong wind tore through

the mountains and broke apart the stones before the LORD. But the LORD wasn't in the wind. After the wind, there was an earthquake. But the LORD wasn't in the earthquake. After the earthquake, there was a fire. But the LORD wasn't in the fire. After the fire, there was a sound. Thin. Quiet. (1 Kings 19:9-12)

There is a beauty and strength to this passage. In his lowest point, Elijah found a strength he never knew he had, he met God is a way that he had never met God before, and he rediscovered his passion for the Lord and for helping God's people remain faithful. In a pit of despair and hopelessness, Elijah experienced God in a profound way that left him with strength for the next leg of his journey. And he saw where he was to go next. God asked Elijah point-blank: "Why are you here?" That is: "Why are you way down *here* in Sinai, at the bottom of the map, when I need you up in the kingdom of Israel?" At the point where Elijah believed he had reached the end of the road, God showed him a new way forward and energized him to follow it.

I don't want to pretend like this kind of thing happens quickly, but low points can leave us with similarly profound experiences of God that help us discover our strength, give us creative insight, and leave us with a passion and vision for our future. Perhaps the most moving example I have seen of this occurred in the lives of two close friends of mine who lost their child to heart disease. The night their sixteen-month-old son died in the hospital, they decided to take some time in the chapel to pray. While there, they had a profound and inexplicable experience of God that gave them a comfort and peace in the midst of an incredibly painful situation. As they grieved the death of their son, they were forced to think creatively about how to live, how to respond, and how to honor both their pain and their son's beautiful legacy. The result was a vision and passion to serve families in similar life circumstances, to spread love, to fight congenital heart disease, and to do their best to see that no one has to go through this pain alone.

It didn't happen overnight, but five years later the couple is thriving, passionately following this vision, and serving others in profound ways. Their newfound purpose doesn't take away the pain of the loss of their son, but that low point has helped them to see the deep strength, creativity, and passion that God has given them. Your low points can reveal your own strength and inner passion as well. Those moments can give you a vision for how you can begin to emerge from your pain and find a new beginning in your own life.

I am sure you could add to this list lessons that you have taken away from low points in your life. Certainly the Israelites were changed at Sinai; there is no denying that. The change that God wrought in their lives, their hearts, their identity, their fortitude, and their character would be needed for the new reality that was ahead. Armed with the Sinai experience, they were ready for their journey to take a different direction. From this point on, the journey would be back up and toward the promised land, the new beginning that God had in store for them.

The same is true for you. This low point doesn't have

to be your last point. In fact, it will not be. It can be your Sinai, your turning point. With patience, faithfulness, and a willingness to show yourself grace and to receive the grace and help of others, you can begin to move through those low points. With a bit of distance, and some perspective, you will begin to see how these moments have changed you, shaped you, and prepared you for a new leg of your own journey. God is not done with you yet. There is something yet ahead, a new land, a new reality, and a new beginning. It is time to turn our eyes in that direction. It is time to leave Sinai, as important as it is, and head back up. God is not done with you or the Israelites. Not yet!

Chapter 8

GIANTS IN THE LAND

—∿∿—

Back when I was planning and preparing to start a church, I met another pastor at a conference who was walking the same road. I was just beginning the process, no more than a month or two into planning it. He had been working on his church-launching project for a year. I remember feeling pretty inadequate after talking with him. He had a detailed business plan, demographic data, a strategic location, great graphics, and printed material, and he even had business cards. All of this impressed me. It looked like he knew what he was doing. He had already met a lot of people in the community where he wanted to start the church. He had connected with local schools and business leaders and seemed to understand the heartbeat of the town. All the pieces were there to start. He had done all the prep work, faithfully followed every step, and attentively planned out and executed a vision to launch. Now, all he had to do was, well, do it!

As we left that conference, I remember being a bit jealous of this fellow pastor. In fact, I met a lot of people at this particular event who seemed much further down the road, with better plans and more specific details about their project than I had. I had a little bit of information and a notepad with some ideas. I had connected with a decent number of people. But I had no money, no location, no website, no brochure or business cards. In fact, I was light on detailed plans, and I realized that I was flying on instinct. That wasn't necessarily a bad thing, but I left feeling a bit insecure.

Fast-forward eighteen months. Though I had left that meeting feeling behind the curve, I went home and got to work. I never developed the detailed plans that some of my colleagues had, but about four months after that conference, The Gathering started weekly worship. It was nerve-wracking for those first few months. We weren't sure if we were going to be able to pay the bills, fill the chairs, and have enough people to serve in our various ministries. We hoped, but didn't know, whether the worship would connect with the new people we were reaching. There was so much that was unknown, but we were going for it. We were doing it. As scary as it was, it was also exhilarating.

Trusting God does not mean that we shouldn't do our due diligence when we are seeking change in our life.

At our one-year anniversary, The Gathering was growing, and we made the decision to start a second worship service. People began to take note of this. Roughly a year and half after I attended that conference, I was invited to another one, this time as a speaker. So I went, and at the event I ran into this same pastor whom I had connected with more than a year earlier. I was excited to hear about the progress of his project and what was happening in his ministry. As we started catching up, he shared with me that he hadn't started weekly worship yet. I was shocked. Over a year ago he had seemed so well prepared. The project had everything it needed. I immediately asked him what had happened.

He started explaining the reasons that he felt they weren't yet ready. He wanted to continue to understand the community, make sure that they had the volunteers they needed, shore up some weak spots in their plans, and launch as strongly as they possibly could. I couldn't argue with some of these sentiments. Being strategic and careful with any bold new step is sensible. I have certainly seen hastiness or poor preparation bring personal and professional visions to a screeching halt. But something didn't seem right.

By this time, the pastor had been working on the project for nearly three years. He had done all the work. He had fastidiously prepared. He had analyzed everything he needed to (and then some). After we talked for about ten minutes, I recognized what I don't think he wanted to admit. He was scared. For so long he had dreamed of starting a new church. When he got the green light, he didn't want to screw up. So he took his time, studied, and prepared his plan. But when it was time to execute, he always found a reason why now wasn't quite the right time. I believe that he was afraid of finally stepping into this dream that, until now, had been just that—a dream. After years of prayers, hard work, sleepless nights, and wilderness wandering, it was time to enter the promised land. And he got cold feet. Perhaps he was scared that it wouldn't work or that he wasn't ready. Maybe he was calling into question his motivation or his purpose. I actually think it was much simpler than all of that. I think he was afraid of failing. So he decided to stay in that proverbial wilderness, making better preparations, studying the situation a bit more, and trying to eliminate every last bit of risk that lay ahead.

I ultimately lost track of that pastor. As far as I'm aware, the project never actually got off the ground. I share this story not to embarrass the pastor or to somehow set myself up as a hero. The truth is that I recognize so well where that guy was coming from because I do the same thing. I get scared of failing, of succeeding, and of everything in between. I share his story because it is something we will all grapple with if we decide to take a risk, follow a call, make a significant change, or migrate from one place in life to an unknown and new place.

It is more common than you think. I've seen many people go through the hardship of leaving behind what is familiar for the sake of something new and promising. I have watched them do the hard work of stepping away from what is comfortable. I have walked alongside them as they move into the unknown terrain of the wilderness. I have sat with them at low points and prayed with them when they weren't sure if this journey was going to lead anywhere. I have lamented and cried with people who never thought they would "arrive" to the place they had hoped and dreamed about. I have seen people do all of this work only to get right on the edge of the new thing, the "promised land," and then become too scared to enter it. After all the work, prayer, planning, preparation, hoping, and dreaming, there is a fear that can often seize us when everything we wanted is finally right in front of us.

THE FEAR OF GETTING TO OUR GOAL

It may sound strange, but as humans, we can actually experience more and more fear the closer we get to the life that we imagined for ourselves. Sometimes we are paralyzed by our very fear of succeeding, of winning, of having the opportunity we have always wanted, or of finally being free of the restraints that hold us back. It doesn't just happen to us; it also happened to Moses and the Israelites, and it happened to Peter when he found himself walking on the water with Jesus. As confusing at it sounds, it is precisely when the Israelites got right up to the border of the promised land, so close that they could climb a peak and look over the river and see it, that they got more scared than at any other point on their journey. After all the work, all the journeying, all the suffering and uncertainty, and traveling, and doubt, when God finally brought them to the place God had promised, they were scared to go in and backed off.

To read this part of the story, we have to hop to a different book of the Bible. The Book of Numbers in the Old Testament is sort of like part two to the exodus story. The Book of Exodus gives us the details of the Israelites' journey out of Egypt, into the wilderness, and down to

Mount Sinai. It essentially ends right after Moses and the Israelites receive all of the laws at Sinai and begin making their ascent, geographically, toward the promised land and, spiritually, out of their low point.

The Book of Numbers takes over after Mount Sinai and covers the second half of the journey. It is worth noting that the wilderness wanderings in Exodus cover a time span (if you include the time at Sinai) of about three to six months; Numbers, however, covers the next thirty-nine-plus years! Needless to say, the journey to the promised land shouldn't have taken that long. This whole trip could have taken under a year. But something went wrong. Numbers tells the story about what exactly happened to the Israelites in the wilderness and why their trip got extended to nearly a half a century.

After leaving Mount Sinai, the Israelites were led by God from that geographic low point north until they reached the desert just south of Canaan (the name of the region that God promised Israel). When they got close to the promised land, God instructed Moses to send leaders from each tribe as spies into the land. The purpose was basic: to get the lay of the new land, to see the challenges that existed and the strength of the foreign powers that they would have to contend with, and to confirm that it was everything God had promised the people. We read about the spies in Numbers 13: "The LORD spoke to Moses: Send out men to explore the land of Canaan, which I'm giving to the Israelites. Send one man from each ancestral tribe, each a chief among them. So Moses sent them out from the Paran desert according to the LORD's command. All the men were leaders among the Israelites" (Numbers 13:1-3).

When the new reality is on the horizon, remember that the journey isn't over. There is going to be work in order to fully transition from wandering in the wilderness to settling in a new place.

I want to stop right here to make a point. Trusting God does not mean that we shouldn't do our due diligence when we are seeking change in our life. This verse reminds us that, when the Israelites arrived in the promised land, the journey was not going to be over. In the new reality, they would face new obstacles, new challenges, and new opportunities. They were still going to need God to direct and guide them. Even though God had promised them the land and was leading them into it, they still had work to do. They had enemies to conquer, cities to build, and a nation to create. They couldn't run headlong into the new reality without planning, preparing, counting the cost, and figuring out a strategy.

I mention this as a kind of counterbalance to the story I started with. The problem with my pastor friend was not that he wanted to plan and prepare. Careful planning is smart. Some of you are planning types; your personality is such that you like to know that you are fully prepared before you do something new. That is a good thing. We will talk about the dangers when that approach becomes too extreme in a little bit. But I also know other people who do little to no planning or preparation. They are content to walk through the wilderness trusting that God will take care of them and lead them. Therefore, they think they do not need to worry about too much. And when the opportunity arises or the time comes for them to seize their opportunity, they hastily jump in, believing that God has their back. For certain people, faith becomes a substitute for preparation, the reason they don't need to worry too much about it or fret too much about the details. This is a mistake and a misunderstanding of the role of faith. Trusting God does not negate the need for sound planning and hard work.

Jesus even talked about this when he told his disciples:

"If one of you wanted to build a tower, wouldn't you first sit down and calculate the cost, to determine whether you have enough money to complete it? Otherwise, when you have laid the foundation but couldn't finish the tower, all who see it will begin to belittle you. They will say, 'Here's the person who began construction and couldn't complete it!' Or what king would go to war against another king without first sitting down to consider whether his ten thousand soldiers could go up against the twenty thousand coming against him? And if he didn't think he could win, he would send a representative to discuss terms of peace while his enemy was still a long way off." (Luke 14:28-32)

Don't use faith as an excuse not to work hard, count the costs, size up the choices in front of you, and tend to the details of your journey. Our contributions to this journey are needed—and expected. God leads, but we still have to follow. God opens doors, but we still have to walk through them. God offers opportunities, but we still have to seize them. God teaches us lessons, but we need to be willing students who learn and grow. God is not a puppet master, and our journey is not artificial. Our decisions, drive, and determination matter. Don't ever allow your faith to let you off the hook from working hard, taking planned risks, and thinking through the changes in your life.

So Moses listened to God, picked the scouts, and sent them off with instructions. He was making careful, wise preparations for the next crucial phase of the journey. As Numbers tells us:

> When Moses sent them out to explore the land of Canaan, he said to them, "Go up there into the arid southern plain and into the mountains. You must inspect the land. What is it like? Are the people who live in it strong or weak, few or many? Is the land in which they live good or bad? Are the towns in which they live camps or fortresses? Is the land rich or poor? Are there trees in it or not? Be courageous and bring back the land's fruit." It was the season of the first ripe grapes. (Numbers 13:17-20)

God had Moses send spies into the land because entering the new reality wasn't going to be a walk in the park. There were people who did not want to coexist with the Israelites and who would fight rather than share their land with tribes they saw as invaders who came from Egypt. There were dangers to consider, logistical challenges with food and resources, and significant work that would be needed before the people could settle in the promised land. The spies were to gather as much information as they could so that the people could be prepared to enter their new home. Of course, God was with them, and the journey would be worth it. But that didn't negate the need for work on their part.

The same is true for us. When the new reality is on the horizon and the opportunity you have been waiting for is finally coming to fruition, remember that the journey isn't over. There is going to be work in order to fully transition from wandering in the wilderness to settling in a new place. Scouting out what the future is going to require and where the pitfalls will be reflects wise planning, not a lack of faith.

Let's not lose sight of the big picture, though. After nearly a year in the wilderness, the Israelites were on the cusp of what they had been praying and waiting for: a land of their own. There is excitement when you finally see the long-sought changes in your life beginning to come into focus. There is an eagerness and readiness to charge ahead. You will need to harness that eagerness and readiness as you make preparations to welcome a new reality in your life. You have to plan, and you have to prepare. But don't lose the enthusiasm. You will need it to overcome the new challenges that await you. At least that is what I have learned from reflecting on what happened next. Because after forty days, the spies returned with news that would stall their journey for a long, long time.

Here's what happened:

> They returned from exploring the land after forty days. They went directly to Moses, Aaron, and the entire Israelite community in the Paran desert at Kadesh. They brought back a report to them and to the entire community and showed them the land's fruit. Then they gave their report: "We entered the land to which you sent us. It's actually full of milk and honey, and this is its fruit. There are, however, powerful people who live in the land. The cities have huge fortifications. And we even saw the descendants of the Anakites there."
>
> (Numbers 13:25-28)

On the positive side, the land was everything that God told the Israelites that it would be. There was rich soil, crops, and abundance. It was truly a land "flowing with milk and honey." But there also were challenges. For starters, powerful people lived in heavily fortified cities with impossibly tall walls. The Israelites would have to contend with these Canaanites and conquer them.

There were even the descendants of the Anakites living in the countryside. The Anakites were a legendary race of giants (think Goliath later on in the biblical story). According to rumors the Israelites had heard, these huge men towered over enemies and were renowned for their abilities in battle. How much truth there was to these claims and about this race of people is a bit fuzzy. But the spies thought they saw these "giants in the land," and we begin to get the sense that they (or at least most of them) were scared. That sense is confirmed just a few verses later when one of the scouts, Caleb, rallies the troops and encouraged them to get ready so that they can take the land:

> Now Caleb calmed the people before Moses and said, "We must go up and take possession of it, because we are more than able to do it." But the men who went up with him said, "We can't go up against the people because they are stronger than we." They started a rumor about the land that they had explored, telling the Israelites, "The land that we crossed over to explore is a land that devours its residents. All the people we saw in it are huge men. We saw there the Nephilim (the descendants of Anak come from the Nephilim). We saw ourselves as grasshoppers, and that's how we appeared to them." (Numbers 13:30-33)

Now we see in full view what would become a struggle over which competing narrative to believe. Two of the ten scouts, Caleb and Joshua (we will talk more about them later), understood the significant challenges and dangers in the new land but believed that the Israelites could overcome them. Significantly, they were the only two scouts who ultimately trusted that God would help them if they continued to move forward wisely but boldly. All of the other scouts had an entirely different narrative, one that gets more fanciful and exaggerated. As they told it, the land was like something out of a horror movie. It *devours* anyone who tries to live there. Now *all* the people are giants. They are not even human anymore. In fact, they described these giants as descendants of humans and angels (the Nephilim, a legendary race of divine/human creatures). Compared to them, the Israelites were mere grasshoppers. There is no way that they could enter this hostile land, much less succeed in taking and settling it.

We can actually get stuck in the wilderness because we get used to the "cover" that the wilderness gives us. The wilderness can make us feel like we are moving forward when in fact we are standing still.

Now I want you to notice something here that I mentioned way back at the beginning of this book. As the scouts told and retold the story, do you see what was happening? The benefits and fruit of the land were no longer seen, no longer even mentioned. All that God had promised about the land was utterly forgotten. There is no mention of why they have come this far and all that God has already helped them overcome (think the splitting of the sea, manna in the wilderness, water from a rock, and the conquering of enemies in the desert). Now, all the scouts could see were the challenges. All they could see were the giants in the land. Not only that, but suddenly the dangers were literally supersized, and they were absolutely insurmountable. These giants were literally and figuratively more than the Israelites believed they can overcome.

After a nearly a year, and with everything they had been through, the Israelites got all the way to the edge of the promised land, and now were too scared to enter. If you keep reading, you find out which narrative wins out. Given the pattern we have seen with the Israelites, you can probably guess. This episode ends with the people making their declaration:

> Then all the congregation raised a loud cry, and the people wept that night. And all the Israelites complained against Moses and Aaron; the whole congregation said to them, "Would that we had died in the land of Egypt! Or would that we had died in this wilderness! Why is the LORD bringing us into this land to fall by the sword? Our wives and our little ones will become booty; would it not be better for us to go back to Egypt?" So they said to one another, "Let us choose a captain, and go back to Egypt."
>
> (Numbers 14:1-4 NRSV)

If you are reading this story all the way through, you almost want to laugh right here. It's kind of comical, really— or maybe tragi-comic would be a better description. And if it seems like I have said that in almost every chapter in this book, it's because it's a definite pattern with the Israelites on their exodus journey. If God were into sending text messages, I have to think that all God would type at this point is SMDH. (If you don't know what that means, ask your kids or Google it.) God has to be thinking, *Seriously? After all I have done for you and with you? After hearing your prayers in Egypt, sending you a leader in Moses, scouring Egypt with plagues, making a path for you through the sea, leading you through the wilderness with fire and cloud, feeding you miraculously in the desert, and providing you water? After giving you a law to live by and forgiving your insolence and lack of faith at Sinai? After promising you a land and then showing you that the promise is ready to become a reality? After all of that, you are scared? After you have seen what I have done, you don't think that I can finish this journey with you? And most of all, instead of even trying, you actually want to turn around and return to slavery? After everything we have been through and nearly a year of journeying, you want to go back to Egypt?*

What follows is not a pretty sight. Despite the protests of Caleb and Joshua and their failed attempts to inspire the people not to make this critical mistake, the people choose to listen to fear instead of trusting God. The scene was so bad that God wanted to disown them right then and there. God even told Moses that he would disinherit them and find a new people to use for this journey. Moses begged and pleaded. In the end, God said that, if the people didn't want to enter the land, then they wouldn't. If they wanted to stay in the desert, then that is where they would stay. The desert would be their home. Then, when all of these people died off, God would lead their children into the land. The only ones from the generation that left Egypt who would go into the new land were the two who trusted, Caleb and Joshua. God granted the rest of the Israelites exactly what they wanted, a life stuck in the desert. For them, it was a disappointing and tragic ending to this journey. But hope had not completely been extinguished. The "people" would eventually make it (at least their kids would). God would lead Israel into the promised land and set them up as their own nation. But it would take a lot longer than anyone thought. Apparently, they weren't ready yet. They weren't ready to fight, and most of all, they weren't ready to courageously trust that God would continue to be with them.

THE FEAR OF GETTING WHAT YOU WANT

There is so much about this part of the story that resonates with any of us who are undergoing transition or change in our life. We don't often think about this fear of a different kind that can take hold of us when our life has the opportunity to change for the better. As much as the wilderness frightens some of us, and as much as that uncertainty and in-between space feels unsatisfying to us, there is a certain safety when we get used to being there. Like the pastor friend at the beginning of this chapter, we can fall back on a safety that is waiting in the form of further study, discernment, and preparation. As long as we are still working on making a change, we don't have to be responsible for the change itself. That is true in business, it is true in our relationships, it is true emotionally, and it is true in our personal lives.

We can actually get stuck in the wilderness because we get used to the "cover" that the wilderness gives us. The wilderness can make us feel like we are moving forward when in fact we are standing still. The wilderness can give us an excuse not to confront our lack of courage. The wilderness can keep us from having to make pivotal decisions by convincing us that we aren't ready yet. The wilderness can lull us into falling in love with research, fact gathering, and analysis, when in reality these become excuses for inaction. The wilderness can give us a convenient reason not to have to face the moment of decision and the impending rush of change that success or failure might bring. In the wilderness, the Israelites could still be works in progress, not having to take ownership of their new future. The wilderness offers us the same convenient way to delay the change, punt the transition a little further down the field, and avoid the seismic changes that even the future we prefer might thrust upon us if it became our present reality.

The wilderness can only teach you so much and prepare you so much. There will come a time when you have to be willing to cross the river, to go through the valley, and to step into the new reality.

Consider again the pastor who, after all of the study, discernment, and planning, was afraid to finally go for it. What do you think the benefits were to waiting? Why was that attractive? Perhaps it gave him more time to minimize the risks. Perhaps there were unplanned contingencies that he felt needed to be worked on. But waiting also allowed him not to have to be accountable for the results of the new project. He could delay finding out if the new reality was going to work. Maybe it was more personal; as long as he was preparing, he wasn't on the hook for having to successfully lead, guide, and manage a new congregation. Perhaps by waiting he could avoid the uncomfortable consequences of potential failure or the massive changes that might come with success. Maybe he actually liked the study and the preparation stage because that played to his gifts. But actually executing the plan scared him because it required him to exercise different muscles. Whatever the reason, the wilderness felt safer to him than the promised land. That was true for Israel as well. It certainly has been true for me, and chances are it will be true for you as well.

Let me offer a different example that may hit close to home for some of you. As I have worked with people in my congregation who have been through great tragedy, pain, or disappointment, I've noticed a pattern. I have worked with several people who have lost spouses prematurely. Grieving the loss of a spouse unexpectedly thrusts people into a long wilderness period. They can never go back to the way life was, and they can't even fathom what life may one day be like. Instead, they need time and space to grieve, process their loss, experience the whole range of emotions that comes with death, and find a new rhythm for living. Oftentimes, this wilderness period may include battling depression, confronting temptations to self-medicate to ease the pain, or trying to avoid the grief that is necessary and healthy. In the wilderness a person may find the help of support groups, begin therapy, and create new transitional support networks to move through the process of losing a life partner. All of this is expected and healthy. There is no right way to grieve and no time line on how long the process might take, but many who do grieve share several of these elements widely.

The grief process is an important one; it is a holy journey out of one reality and toward a new one that is meant to neither replace nor supersede the old. It is a migration from one way of living to an entirely new one. Along with the similarities and patterns that I have noted above, there is another one that I have often observed. After spending a significant amount of time in the wilderness, grieving in healthy ways, they may have an opportunity to move into a new relationship. For some, this day might never come. Maybe they don't desire a new relationship. But most of the time, after some amount of grief (the timetable ranges from months to decades), these people find themselves at least interested in exploring a new relationship. They begin to contemplate what it might feel like to experience the joy of that kind of companionship again. While this is a beautiful transition that in some ways marks a significant step on the grief journey, it is one that can immediately scare people.

There is a sense in which contemplating a new relationship means forgetting the lost spouse. Guilt can arise from experiencing happiness again. Sometimes the person forms a strong identity as a grieving widower or widow, along with a community of people who are walking that road together. Starting a new relationship can in some ways feel like giving up or at least diminishing that status. For many people, the thought of moving fully into a new relationship scares them, not because the relationship might fail, but because it might succeed. What if they are suddenly happy again? What if their grief isn't as acute as it once was? What if their dead spouse is no longer always at the forefront of their mind? What if they find themselves happier than they have ever been before? Does this somehow dishonor or negate the love they had for their first partner?

Because of these kinds of questions and others, people are often tempted to stop short of that new reality. They stay frozen in a certain stage of grief for a complex constellation of reasons. They can actually grow comfortable being in a certain stage, and they can begin to use their grief as a convenient reason not to move forward or risk new relationships. This isn't always true, of course. But for many people, the fear of transitioning to a new place in life keeps them stuck in a cycle of grief that can become unhelpful and unhealthy or that can hold them back from future happiness. They can find themselves trapped in the wilderness, not able to go back, but forever unready to move forward.

This isn't just true with grief or starting a new enterprise; it can be true in virtually every aspect of our life. We can adapt and find comfort in the wilderness of life, so much so that we find ourselves fearful of ever moving out of it. Sometimes it can look like paralysis by analysis. Other times, the wilderness is more about the avoidance of hard questions. For some, the wilderness gives them reason to forever claim a kind of "victim mentality." The wilderness and its richness for learning and discovering yourself can become distorted so that more learning, more maturing, and more self-discovery really become thinly veiled excuses for not taking new risks and not owning new consequences. The wilderness can give us a reason to stop short, giving up on our initial dream because it now seems too lofty, too risky, too bold, or fraught with too many "giants." Suddenly, staying in the wilderness can make it feel like we have "come far enough." We may allow ourselves to believe that, as long as we don't go back to Egypt, it is OK just to stop right here. This way, we can claim a partial victory without having the hard work and challenges of the new promised land.

All of these dynamics and more were at work for the Israelites. If you read the rest of Numbers, you find that the Israelites begin truly wandering around the wilderness. They literally journey in circles, occasionally coming back by the promised land, peering into it, and deciding once again the time isn't right or the risks are too great. They always come up with a new reason why one more lap in the wilderness will help them be better prepared or more able to conquer the challenges that await them. The truth is that the wilderness has now become safe. At first, the wilderness can transform us in all kinds of important ways by teaching us, tempting us, shaping us, and readying us for the stage ahead. But over time, if we overstay our welcome, one more lap around the wilderness is not teaching us anything new, preparing us any better, or eliminating any risks. The wilderness is no longer helping us become who we need to be to enter the new reality. Instead, it is becoming a convenient excuse not to have to face the beauty, challenge, adventure, and work that another transition would require of us.

That is what happened to Israel, at least for that first generation of Israelites. They needed about a year of wilderness time for God to shape them and prepare them. The other thirty-nine years were on them. The other thirty-nine were the price they were willing to pay for their fear of finally taking hold of what they were being prepared for. They decided that settling in the wilderness was a price worth paying for not having to face their giants, scale what looked like impossibly high walls, and find out if they had what it takes to complete the journey. In many ways, it is a sad end to the Israelites' individual stories. These were the people brave enough to face down Pharaoh's army, risk-taking enough to cross a splitting sea, and tough enough to march through the desert. But the narrative of fear of the new reality and their own inadequacies to overcome the challenges won out.

What happened to the Israelites serves as a warning for all of us that the wilderness can be a tempting stopping point. It is easy to shoot for the stars but stop in the front lawn. It is easy to commit to running a marathon but then decide that a 5K will do after taking a look at the work and commitment a marathon demands (not that there is anything wrong with a 5K, mind you—I've never run a marathon!). My point is that it can be easy to stop short and decide that the wilderness is far enough. But what makes me so sad is that the promised land was *right there*. It was just across the valley, right on the other side of the river. Right over there was a life far beyond what the Israelites could have imagined, a life flowing with milk and honey. The only reason the first generation of Israelites didn't get to experience it was because they listened to the voice of fear in their heads. They overestimated the obstacles, and they underestimated themselves and the God who led them. I don't want the same thing to happen to me. I don't want it to happen to you, either.

There are always going to be "giants in the land" and walls that look impossible to scale. A transition into a new job, a new relationship, a new lifestyle, or a new chapter in your business, church, or organization is always going to tempt us to highlight the risks and challenges while minimizing the promise and potential. Don't let the narrative of fear take over. You have overcome so much to get where you are. With God's help you have already scaled impossibly high walls. By God's grace you have already conquered immensely powerful adversaries—emotionally, spiritually, and figuratively. In the end, the wilderness can only teach you so much and prepare you so much. There will come a time when you have to be willing to cross the river, to go through the valley, and to step into the new reality. You can, and you will. You've got this. You were made for this. As the old Nike ad says, it is time to "just do it."

Chapter 9

CROSSING THE RIVER

—◦◦◦—

*C*ourage. That word is a bit old-fashioned; at least that is how it sounds to me. It seems like something you associate with people who accomplish incredible feats in the face of great obstacles. Young civil rights marchers facing down police during the march from Selma to Montgomery, troops taking the beach at Normandy, or firefighters running into a collapsing skyscraper on 9/11: those are the kinds of acts we think of as courageous. Courage is displayed by people who are larger than life, people whom we read about in a textbooks or watch on the History Channel.

But courage is not limited to larger-than-life characters. It is a Christian virtue practiced every day by ordinary women, men, and children. Courage is not limited to the well-trained, the well-prepared, or the well-resourced. Courage is not a function of education, class, race, or wealth. Courage isn't doled out in ultralimited doses to a few lucky people each generation, and it isn't a top-secret attribute that can only be unlocked by a few. Every day, in millions of small ways—and over a lifetime in a few big ways—all of us have the opportunity to choose courage. Every time we face a life situation, a change, a transition, a pain in our life, a problem, an injustice, or a tragedy, we have the opportunity for courage. And if you are going to follow Jesus, if you are going to commit your life to being part of God's work in the world, you will need courage every single day.

We don't always think of faith as involving courage. We list familiar attributes like faith, hope, and love as the signs of a life with God. But we should include courage. Paul, an apostle and principal leader in the early church, reminded his protégé, Timothy, of this in a letter: "for God did not give us a spirit of cowardice, but rather a spirit of power" (2 Timothy 1:7 NRSV).

And in a letter to Christians in the ancient Greek city of Corinth, Paul said this of all Christ-followers: "Keep alert, stand firm in your faith, be courageous, be strong" (1 Corinthians 16:13 NRSV).

One of the biggest myths I run into when it comes to faith is that, when we decide to invite God into our lives, when we listen to God's call, and when we follow Jesus, somehow life gets easier. That it is always better. That the hard stuff melts away and we no longer have to face adversity, injustice, pain, tragedy, or serious challenge. We imagine that God is like a force field that keeps us from all hardship in this world. It's not true. It's not even close to true.

God is present. Absolutely. God protects and provides. God leads us and promises us a victory in the end. But God never promises that life will not be hard, that following will not come with serious setbacks and challenges. In fact, God knows the journey will be hard. It will be hard in the beginning when you are deciding to make a change, hard in the middle when you are stuck between the old and the new, and hard even when you enter that new reality, the "promised land." There is no place this side of heaven that doesn't require us to stand strong, to take heart, and to be courageous. This isn't supposed to be easy. Change isn't supposed to be a walk in the park. Transformation is difficult, and if you are looking for a pain-free path from Egypt to the promised land, from where you are to where God is calling you to be, then you are on the wrong bus. Faith is hard, and it requires courage.

Like the Israelites, we struggle with God. Sometimes, God has to lead us by the roundabout route through the wilderness. But God is with us on every step of our journey.

Good thing, then, that courage is a choice. It's a good thing that there are no prerequisites for courage or barriers to entry. Good thing you have courage and that you can choose it right now, today. You're going to need it. That is the hard news. But the good news is that, because of God, you have it and can choose it. As I said when we started the journey, you've got this. I'll say it again as we come to the end. It isn't going to get easier, just because the new reality is right in front of you. It doesn't get easier when we finally find ourselves emerging into a new and hoped-for future. It doesn't get easier just because we have migrated from Egypt to a new place. But it can be better. But it is going to take courage.

Courage is where we started, when the Israelites had to make the choice to leave Egypt, the only home they had ever known. It required bravery to step away from a familiar and predictable life to step into the wilderness. It took courage to trust God to lead in the midst of a wilderness journey that looked anything but planned. And now that Israel is on the cusp of the promised land, it is not surprising that it will take courage for them to enter it.

It is interesting that the exodus story begins and ends with water. To leave Egypt, the Israelites had to muster up the courage and faith to step into the Red Sea, trusting that God would indeed part it before them and deliver them from the hands of Pharaoh. As we talked about earlier, the legend of Nahshon was moving precisely because that journey would never have begun if it weren't for his willingness to take the first step. It is fitting then that the story of the exodus formally concludes with a new generation of Israelites, raised in the wilderness that had been their home for forty years, standing on the banks of the Jordan River, fearful and scared of crossing over it into a land that God had promised their parents. They, too, had a leader. Like Moses leading the people before him (and Nahshon who was willing to take a first step), this time it was Joshua whose faith and courage compelled the Israelites to cross that river.

WHY WAS MOSES LEFT BEHIND?

In the previous chapter, we left the story of the Israelites in the desert. After refusing to enter the land because of their fear, the people finally had pushed God to the limit. In anger, God told Moses that he would strike the people with a plague and raise up a different chosen nation, one that would be stronger and more faithful. Moses begged God to stick with Israel, even though Israel would not listen to God. Here's how God gave his verdict to Moses: "None of you who were enlisted and were registered from 20 years old and above, who complained against me, will enter the land in which I promised to settle you, with the exception of Caleb, Jephunneh's son, and Joshua, Nun's son. But your children, whom you said would be taken by force, I'll bring them in and they will know the land that you rejected" (Numbers 14:29b-31).

In many ways it was a creative solution. God would continue to keep his promise to Israel, but a generation would need to pass. If the adults wouldn't enter the land, God would wait for their children. The next generation, without the same experiences, fears, and expectations, would be in a better position to do what their parents could not.

On top of this, many who read the story of the exodus are surprised to find out that even Moses, the fearless leader of the Israelites since their time in slavery—the one who talked with God on the mountain, and the prophet who brought the law to the people—would not be allowed to enter the land. This seems strange to those of us who have followed Moses's faithfulness this entire story. We never read of Moses wishing to go back to Egypt. We never read of Moses losing trust in God. We can understand why God did not allow the rest of that generation to cross into Canaan, but what did Moses do to deserve this fate?

The answer is in Numbers 20, which describes another drought and tells us how the people were afraid they would die of thirst (this is another repeating plot point in the story). Moses received instructions from God to call forth water from a rock. Moses did so, but not precisely in the way God wanted. For this, God said, Moses could not enter the land. This seems like a strange and extreme punishment. While scholars and biblical interpreters argue over the exact nature of Moses's mistake, the outcome is the same. Moses and the adult Israelites who left Egypt would not be the ones who enter the promised land (save Caleb and Joshua).

I bring all of this up because one major question many people have is, Why? If God is supposed to be faithful, steadfast, and loyal, why would God punish the people in this way? Is God going to leave us in the wilderness to die as well? That would be a decidedly uninspiring end to this book! So I need to take a moment to talk about this part of the story and how it might inform our own journey.

When we read the scripture, it is easy to forget that the assumptions and contexts were much different than ours are today. This is a story in which the primary character is a nation, Israel. Now, there are important people along the way, like Moses. But the promise God made was to a people, the journey was about a people, and the whole story of scripture is about how God is using this chosen people to change the world. In our culture, and even when it comes to faith, we often think about the individual first. How does something apply to me? What is God doing for me or in my life? That was not the primary question in the Bible.

Instead, the focus is on what God is doing for God's people as a whole.

But remember something about the stories of God's chosen people. God's promise to make these people into a great nation was delivered to Abram (Abraham). But the people did not come to be called Abraham-ites. God's covenant with the people was passed down through Abraham's son, Isaac. But the people are not called Isaac-ites. God renewed the covenant through Isaac's son, Jacob. But Jacob's descendants were not known as Jacob-ites. That's because God changed Jacob's name to Israel, which means "the one who struggles with God." The story of the Israelites in the Bible is the story of people who struggle with God. They struggle to be faithful. They struggle to be obedient to God's command to love God with all their heart and to love their neighbors, their fellow children of God. But God never abandons the promise. Amid their struggles, God is always with them.

That's how we fit into the story. Like the Israelites, we struggle with God. Sometimes, God has to lead us by the roundabout route through the wilderness. But God is with us on every step of our journey.

Given this context, it is not surprising that one generation of Israel made it from Egypt to the wilderness while another made it from the wilderness to the promised land. Similarly, the story wouldn't end there. Several more generations would have to come and go in order for Israel to be forged into a nation. One generation would build a temple, another would reject God and lead to its destruction, and yet another would have to rebuild it. The individuals change, but the story of God's faithfulness to Israel, despite their rebellion, stubbornness, and sin, continues throughout the whole Bible. It is that story that has its fulfillment in Christ and is offered to each person in Jesus's name.

THE JOURNEY IS THE DESTINATION

When we read this part of the story and think about these differences between contexts, it reminds me of a few important truths. First, all of us are part of something bigger than ourselves. Our lives, at least if we want to follow Jesus, are not merely our own. That is not to say there isn't space for our individual hopes, desires, and intentions. But we ought to remember that our story is part of a larger story about what God is doing. We get to be a part of it, and that is incredible! It doesn't begin with us or end with us, but that doesn't minimize our role in it. Just as Moses, when he followed in faith, had an important part to play in God's plans, so we, too, can play a critical role in God's story if we have the faith and trust to follow God's leading.

Second, thinking about some of the Israelites not making it to the promised land reminds me that some parts of who I am must be left behind if I am to embrace the new future that God is always calling me toward. Think of yourself as Israel for just a minute. Just as part of Israel—the unfaithful part, the untrusting part, the disobedient part—had to be left behind in the wilderness, so it is with each of us. We cannot simultaneously embrace change and transition in our life *and* not leave certain attitudes behind, put certain habits to bed, or allow certain behaviors to die. The wilderness is a time for refinement when we must learn who we are and who we are to become in order to do what God is calling us to do. Parts of each of us die anytime we go through a God-led transition. It is a hard but true reality.

Just because we arrive at a new reality or a new beginning doesn't mean the journey suddenly stops or the road suddenly becomes easy.

But the longer we sit with the Israelites and Moses, the more we realize that in many ways the destination was the journey. It was their journey that taught them to trust God. It was the journey that shaped them into the people they became. It was the journey that refined them, challenged them, consoled them, rewarded them, frustrated them, and inspired them. They ultimately became the people God wanted them to become because of the journey. Yes, on this side of heaven they didn't get to experience everything they had hoped to. But they grew and they set the stage for the next generation to continue to advance.

To get back to our story, Deuteronomy ends with Moses climbing up another mountain. This one was called Nebo, and it was on the east side of the Jordan River. From there, God showed Moses the promised land that lay beyond the river. Moses could see it, feel it, almost reach out and touch it. He wouldn't get to enter it. But he was able to reach the end of his life knowing that he had done his job. He had led the people to the place God had intended. He had fulfilled his task and stayed faithful to his call. Because of that, the Israelites would one day become the people God intended them to be. Moses would go down as the greatest prophet. In fact, the Book of Deuteronomy ends with a simple tribute: "No prophet like Moses has yet emerged in Israel; Moses knew the LORD face-to-face! That's not even to mention all those signs and wonders that the LORD sent Moses to do in Egypt—to Pharaoh, to all his servants, and to his entire land—as well as all the extraordinary power that Moses displayed before Israel's own eyes!" (Deuteronomy 34:10-12).

Moses lived life well, and faith took him on an adventure that changed the course of his life and the course of history. He could have died an old man tending to his sheep in Midian. But because he trusted, because he listened to the call and followed the nudge, because he had the courage to leave home, to step out, to risk, and to wander, he got to play a role in God's story. Moses didn't enter the land, but he experienced a life far beyond anything he could have imagined. All because he was willing to go.

Israel's story generally—and Moses's story in particular—reminds me of a quote by the twentieth-century theologian Reinhold Niebuhr: "Nothing that is worth doing can be achieved in our lifetime; therefore we must be saved by hope."

I am reminded here of the words spoken by Dr. Martin

Luther King Jr. on the night before he died; he invoked the image of Moses on Mount Nebo. Dr. King was a leader of people whose ancestors, like the Israelites, had known the horror of slavery. And in the century since the formal end of slavery in the United States, they had endured incredible hardship and oppression fueled by the sin of racism that infected their fellow Americans. They were engaged in a great struggle. And while they had come far, the people had not witnessed the realization of Dr. King's dream of a time when all people would be judged not "by the color of their skin but by the content of their character."

On that fateful night in Memphis, Dr. King told the crowd that had gathered in a church that he might not live long enough to reach the goal with them, but that the goal was in sight, and they would get there if they kept walking together in faith. "I have been to the mountaintop," he said, "and I have seen the promised land."

It would be pretentious to believe that we will personally complete every mission, make every change, and finish every work that we begin. We won't. Sometimes that is because of our own effort (or lack thereof). Sometimes, we will change directions. In some endeavors we will fail. Sometimes, we simply go as far as we can and have to be content to pass the baton to someone else. We must rely on faith and hope.

At the edge of the promised land, Moses passed the baton to his protégé, Joshua. In front of God and the people, Moses transferred the mantle of leadership. It is a significant and beautiful moment. Joshua has been by Moses's side for decades. Joshua was with him on Sinai and was one of the spies who entered the promised land nearly forty years earlier. While the people failed to trust and believe in God, Joshua is described as always faithful, always trusting, always encouraging the Israelites to move forward not back. Now it was up to him to lead the people on the final step of this particular journey, and so it is with Joshua that we will end our story.

But, predictably, before they could cross the river into the promised land, Joshua and the people had to face down their old enemy one more time. They were on the shores of the Jordan, just a small river separating them from everything that God has promised. The only thing standing in their way was what has always stood in their way: fear.

BE STRONG AND VERY COURAGEOUS

If the forty-year exodus story were a movie, this would be the climactic scene. In the decades since they left Egypt, the Israelites have witnessed miracles, faced down death, conquered enemies, and learned the hard way to rely on God. Now, their children were on the banks of the Jordan River, ready to cross into the land that was promised to their parents. The children certainly knew the stories of their parents' disobedience. They likely grew up listening to tales of the beauty of the land that they were to inherit, but also to the rumors of fearsome giants and insurmountable obstacles. They would have learned fear. Almost certainly, they would have heard from their elders that the promised land, while wonderful, was not a realistic possibility. In this way, even fear is generational, limiting what is possible before children even have the ability to recognize it. Fear is invasive. If it isn't confronted, it spreads and becomes part of the lens through which we and those who come after us see the world.

All this is to say that fear doesn't go away unless it is confronted. If fear sounds like a familiar refrain by now, as if it keeps cropping up in every stage of the journey of this story, then you have been paying attention. The Israelites had a lot of challenges, a lot of enemies, and a lot of significant obstacles to overcome. But underneath all of them was fear.

So it makes sense that, as the second generation out of Egypt stood on the plains of Moab staring across the Jordan River at this storied land of Canaan, they felt the fear of their parents rising within them. If Joshua was going to lead them across to possess what was promised, and to begin their new story, he would have to convince them to take courage.

The first chapter of the Book of Joshua is really a manifesto about courage. As a whole, the book is all about the challenges and promise of the new land. It would be a good part 2 to this book. Just because we arrive at a new reality or a new beginning doesn't mean the journey suddenly stops or the road suddenly becomes easy. Any of you who have undertaken a significant new venture and successfully managed major transitions in your life know that the fear never goes away. There is always something just ahead that, if you let it, can let loose a whole new round of fear. But as long as we are focused on the fear, we never get very far, and we can miss out on what God really wants to do in our lives. If the Israelites want to see the promised land, and if they want to experience the fullness of the life God wanted for them, they had to conquer their fear and cross the river.

It is the same for each of us. Your greatest enemy on your journey, your biggest obstacle, and your most insurmountable challenge is not out there; it is inside you. It is your fear. If I were to list all the fears I see at play in us, I could fill up several volumes. But let me just share the ones that I think plague us most often. We have talked in part about each of these, but I want to name them once again so you recognize them.

FEAR OF LOSS

This is really about our instinct to avoid grief for ourselves and shield others from it. Fear of loss crops up at every stage of our journey. But it is most pronounced at the transition points—when we finally have to leave Egypt and step into the wilderness, and then again when we finally have to step from the wilderness into a new reality. Every transition—even those we desire—comes with a loss. We fear losing what we currently have. As I have worked with people, I have seen a few contributing factors to this fear. First is our own uncertainty that what we lose now will be replaced by what comes next.

Second, we live in a culture that tempts us to believe that we can have it all. That we don't have to make sacrifices or trade-offs. That we can somehow find solutions in life that allow us to change without changing or move forward without leaving anything behind. I see this especially with organizations and businesses. There is a desire to shield people from grief, and we pretend as if we can hold on to the current reality while also pursuing a transition. We do this to make people feel better or lessen the sting of loss. But often we only exacerbate the problem. When we avoid allowing people to experience the impact of a loss, then we inadvertently stunt their ability to move on and embrace a new reality.

I have the opportunity to visit a lot of churches and see the evidence of this kind of deal-making all over the place. I often get asked by leaders, "How do we change to reach new people while still pleasing the people who are here?" Or they'll ask, "How can we keep what we have and value it while at the same time working for change and adding ministries or programs that will speak to new generations of people?" I have thought a lot about these kinds of questions. I'd like to be able to reply that there is some kind of magic bullet that will help a church to change. But I can't. I think it is disingenuous to pretend that you can stay and go, change and remain the same, have your cake and eat it too. It is unrealistic to think that you can move forward and live into a new reality without losing *something*. Loss is a hallmark of transition. So when we try to avoid it, we usually avoid the change itself. As leaders we are often so allergic to allowing our people simply to grieve that we attempt to "solve" their loss. In the process, we often retreat from the very changes that we believed God was calling us to make.

In our lives, the same principle holds true. It is OK to lose certain realities in your life. It is OK to grieve about them. It is OK for change to hurt and for us to feel the sting of loss about what we are leaving behind. Jesus talked about this challenge with those who would follow him. He was realistic about the hard concessions that following him would entail. He didn't pull punches or protect people from having to make those hard decisions: "Someone else said to Jesus, 'I will follow you, Lord, but first let me say good-bye to those in my house.' Jesus said to him, 'No one who puts a hand on the plow and looks back is fit for God's kingdom'" (Luke 9:61-62).

Courage means allowing yourself to let go and lose in order to move forward and gain new realities in your life. Courage is allowing yourself to feel that hurt, process it, and move through it while holding onto the hope that God has something prepared for you. Courage is not allowing your fear of loss to hold you back from moving forward. Courage is leading people by naming their loss, allowing them to grieve, and not trying to fix the loss.

As the Israelites stood on the banks of the Jordan, Joshua couldn't pretend that life was going to be unalterably different if they crossed that river. He was honest about the challenges and forthright about the new reality. Courage was allowing people to name what they were going to lose but leading them forward anyway.

FEAR OF FAILURE

A second fear that consistently crops up in our story (and in the larger story of the Israelites and all of us who "struggle with God") is the fear of failure. Sometimes this takes the form of literally dying—at the hands of Pharaoh, of starvation in the wilderness, or by the spears of an opposing army. While our fear of failure usually doesn't include physical death (though in some cases it can), it hinders our attempts to manage change. I see this all the time in my own story. When I want to try something new or I want to take a risk or I want to follow a God-inspired nudge in my life, immediately I begin to think about "what if." What if it doesn't work out? What if I don't have what it takes? What will happen to my career, reputation, or relationships if I fall short? What if this exposes me as not knowing what I am doing? What if this new step is more than I can manage or mitigate? Gradually, and then all at once, I can "what if" a new idea to death, before I even start.

My fear of inadequacy, my fear of not being liked, my fear of not being good enough, my fear of missing the expectations that others have of me and for me—all of these are, in one form or another, a fear of failing. As I get older, I think to some extent this is a progressive fear as well. The older we get, the more we have to lose, the more "realistic" we become, and the more we value safety and security. It is not universal, but I see it in enough people that it bears naming. We see it in the story of Israel, most clearly when they were afraid of the new beginning because all they could see was what might go wrong instead of what might be gained.

When I speak to church pastors and leaders, they often ask, "If you could do anything over again, what would you do differently?" My response is the same every time.

"Early in my ministry," I say, "I spent so much time worrying about failing that I didn't think at all about what might happen if I succeeded. I was so focused on not failing that I was not focused on thriving."

This may not sound like a big deal, but I believe that I actually missed early miracles and work that God wanted to do in and with me precisely because I was thinking too small. If our goal becomes not failing, we are forever playing a defensive game in life. We approach every change, call, or transition from a deficit standpoint—what we might lose instead of what might be gained. This keeps us from the abundant life that God wants for us, the overflowing kind of life that God imagines for us.

Courage is sometimes the willingness to choose a course of action and throw ourselves into it wholeheartedly, trusting that, by following the call, it will lead us to the place God intends us to be.

To add to all of this, our fear of failure comes from a fundamentally false assumption that failure always and only *hurts* us. But most of us, when we are able to look back at moments of failure in our lives, can recognize that even in those worst-case scenarios we learned, grew, were shaped by God, and were prepared for the future. We simply overestimate the cost of failing and underestimate the cost of never trying.

When the Israelites were standing on the shore looking across that river, Joshua had to keep them focused on the vision, the picture of the future that God had imagined for them. The more they focused on that, the less time they had to focus on their fears of what might happen if they didn't succeed. Ultimately it worked, and Joshua was able to lead them across. Perhaps they knew all too well from watching their parents that the fear of failing was not worth giving up what God had prepared for them.

Courage is recognizing that failure is a real possibility and yet stepping out, trusting that God can indeed weave together all we do for our ultimate good. It is recognizing that in God's care, painful failure is also a refining process that shapes us. Courage is keeping our eyes focused on what we could win by trusting.

FEAR OF COMMITMENT

You may know this fear by a different name. It is often called FOMO or the fear of missing out. This may sound like a strange fear to name, but I often see it holding people back in their journey with God. There is a lot of popular wisdom that points to a decline in commitment in our culture. If you don't believe me, just send out an invitation that requires an RSVP. You might be surprised how many people just don't do it (or wait until the absolute last minute). What is going on with this?

I think it is fundamentally a fear of committing to one

course of action or decision. There is a sense that, by committing, we restrict our options. Then if something more enticing, or "better," comes along, we will be left out. So we make a decision that seems to make sense to us. We keep our options open. That way, we can be flexible, adaptable, and evolving. We think that we will be more able to respond to developing opportunities in our life.

It seems to make sense and almost seems to be wise. I believe it is actually a deep-seated fear that does not work to our advantage. The misunderstanding begins with a misconception about commitment. We think of commitment as restrictive, like a loss of freedom and options. Commitment conjures up images of loss and the closing of future possibilities. Commitment sounds exclusive, that by picking one thing we are necessarily saying no to myriad other possibilities. Therefore, we shy from choosing a course of action. Decisions can seem, well, so *decisive*. There is a sense that we cannot turn back from them.

While that view is not totally wrong, it also misses the bigger picture. Here is what we are not seeing. When we perennially attempt to keep our options open to all things, we ensure that we will miss out on *every* thing. The fear of missing out, oddly, leads to missing out! Think of it in terms of a Saturday night commitment. Let's say you receive an invitation to a party. It sounds fun, some people you know will be there, and you think you may want to go. But you aren't sure what your others friends are doing. They may be hanging out or going out, and you'd likely enjoy that more. So you wait. You don't commit. You have a few up-in-the-air possibilities but no solid plans. You'll figure it out, just go with the flow. Suddenly, Saturday night arrives. One friend bails out on some potential plans, another has to work, and the options you once imagined don't materialize. It's getting late and you throw in the towel. You waited so long thinking that you would have choices that, in the end, you didn't go anywhere.

Now I know this is low stakes. But I see it happen to people at all levels of life. In an effort to keep our options open we miss out on the best opportunities God presents to us. We stall, we tell ourselves "not yet," and we imagine that we have plenty of time. As a result, the opportunities to seize new promises and start new beginnings pass us by.

It is the God of heaven and earth who created you, calls you, loves you, forgives you, strengthens you, and walks with you. You are not alone.

I think this is part of what happened to the Israelites when they started circling in the desert. Committing to crossing over, deciding to go for it, always seemed so definitive. It was easier for them to analyze, consider, take a little more time, and circle around the wilderness yet again. They literally died because they couldn't decide that maybe today was the day to go for it.

Let's not let the same thing happen to us. Courage is sometimes the willingness to choose a course of action and throw ourselves into it wholeheartedly, trusting that, by following the call, it will lead us to the place God intends us to be. We cannot spend all of our time considering what we are missing. Courage is the ability to tune out the other options, keep ourselves from "the grass is greener" thinking, and commit ourselves to God. Courage is letting go of the fear of missing out and instead recognizing that the only way to meaningful living is by making intentional choices to do what we believe God is calling us to do.

FEAR OF CRITICISM

This fear can also be a fear of embarrassment, looking silly, seeming weird, not being normal, or losing face with people we respect. Basically, this is the fear of what people might think of us because of the decisions we make or the path we choose to follow. Jesus once said: "Go in through the narrow gate. The gate that leads to destruction is broad and the road wide, so many people enter through it. But the gate that leads to life is narrow and the road difficult, so few people find it" (Matthew 7:13-14).

Think about these words for a minute. On the one hand, the gate and road that lead to authentic and abundant life are narrow, and you don't have to worry about a lot of traffic. There are few people who choose that road. On the other hand, the road that leads to destruction is wide, crowded, and busy. If you follow the crowd, or live your life seeking the approval of the majority of people around you, which path do you suppose you'll end up taking? You guessed it. Not the narrow one. Not the less-traveled one. If life change and meaningful transition were easy, everyone would do it willingly. But it is not easy, and so it often looks crazy to the person who is comfortably ensconced in Egypt.

When you step out and try something new in your life—or when you, through prayerful discernment, decide to follow a call that you believe has come from God—your decision is going to look silly (or worse) to at least a few people in your life. I remember having to sit down with my parents at an Applebee's near my college to inform them that, after four years of college, I had decided what I wanted to do with my life. They waited eagerly. For four years of college I couldn't ever name what I actually wanted to do. They had invested big money in an ultraexpensive private university. It was time to finally see what it was that I had come up with. So I told them.

"I think I want to be a pastor."

There was a pause, a long silence, and then my father said, quite stoically, "If you knew you wanted to be a pastor, you could have picked a cheaper school."

That was true. I was scared to tell them about this decision because I knew they would think I was a little bit crazy. Hell, I thought I was a little bit crazy. Who majors in theoretical math at an expensive university only to decide to go be a pastor? No one. I have to say in full disclosure that my parents rapidly came around and were very supportive. Today, they attend my church, and I generally believe they are proud of the path that I am pursuing! But the feeling I had before talking with them sticks with me. It was repeated in countless conversations I had during my senior year of college. From friends to professors, to people whom I respected in my life, I just knew they thought my decision was a little out there. Even a career counselor at my university said something that almost caused me to change my mind. Upon telling her that I thought I knew what I wanted to do, and shared with her my decision to go to seminary, she responded, "Well, that would be a waste."

Ouch. That one hurt. Maybe it was a waste. Maybe I was silly, or naive, or downright ignorant of life and work and the realities of picking a career that actually matters. They could have been right. It wasn't as if their advice was necessarily bad or that they shared it with ill intent. But here's the thing: they weren't right. They were wrong. My choice wasn't naive, and it wasn't stupid. Most of all, it was not a waste. One more aside, I felt vindicated when, fifteen years after that career counselor told me I was wasting my time and talents, my university alumni magazine called to write a story about The Gathering in a series of articles on interesting careers people ended up pursuing.

In hindsight, my choice was not silly. I know that I vetted it, prayed about it, and talked it through with people whose opinions I respected. I know it wasn't hasty. If I had listened to the naysayers or had been overly concerned with what others thought about me, I never would have done it. I tell this story because, to this day, bold decisions, new ventures, and fresh calls from God still bring up this same reaction in others and the same fear within me.

I'm not saying that you should make rash choices. Don't ignore all sound advice and close yourself off from the perspective of others. But also do not let the opinions of others be the guiding principle for your journey. Needing to please others, avoid criticism, or assuage critics is not a good way to make decisions. All this will do is ensure that you are on the wide, crowded, and easy road, one that leads to nothing new, nothing interesting, and nothing truly creative.

The Israelites consistently complained to Moses about the apparent stupidity of their choice to simply follow a pillar of cloud through a barren wilderness. They constantly chided Moses on the foolishness of believing they could conquer a foreign army or scale the walls of fortified cities. On the shores of the Jordan River that day, Joshua had to convince them that nothing truly great was accomplished without the criticism and snickers of a peanut gallery. Courage is recognizing that sometimes you cannot be concerned with pleasing the people around you or avoiding looking foolish to people you respect. Sometimes, the right thing, the authentic and faithful decision, is a lonely one. Courage is the willingness to do it anyway.

CROSSING OVER

With the fear welling up inside of them, the Israelites camped on the banks of the Jordan opposite the promised land. God visited Joshua, just as he had visited Moses all those many times. God offered a promise to him: "No one will be able to stand up against you during your lifetime. I will be with you in the same way I was with Moses. I won't desert you or leave you. Be brave and strong, because you are the one who will help this people take possession of the land, which I pledged to give to their ancestors" (Joshua 1:5-6).

I hope you read those words as applying to you. God created you. God loves you. God has a purpose for you and wants to use you to influence and affect others. God is not finished with you, and you are not defined by your past. There is a journey ahead, and God wants to lead you. It may seem crazy, and the change may feel like more than you can bear. You are going to be scared. That is all part of the journey. But you've got this. You can do this. This is what it always feels like to manage God-inspired change and healthy transition in life. You are not doing it alone. If you were, then maybe you would have something to worry about. But you are not alone.

The last words Jesus ever said to his disciples in the Gospel of Matthew are eerily similar to the words God shared with Joshua that day: "Look, I myself will be with you every day until the end of this present age" (Matthew 28:20b).

It is the God of heaven and earth who created you, calls you, loves you, forgives you, strengthens you, and walks with you. You are not alone. I will close with God's summary to Joshua, a reminder of all that God has already said, and a simple mantra for Joshua and all of us to live by in the future: "I hereby command you: Be strong and courageous; do not be frightened or dismayed, for the LORD your God is with you wherever you go" (Joshua 1:9).

Conclusion

FOR ALL THE JOURNEYS AHEAD

—‹⁄⁄›—

You may not be surprised to learn that the Israelites' story wasn't over after they crossed the Jordan River. The crossing was a new beginning and a major milestone in their journey. But another leg of their journey with God was just starting. Just as they imagined, the promised land held new challenges and obstacles, and they would still have to contend with the same old fears that had plagued them in the wilderness. But they were not the same people. They had grown, learned, and developed strengths during their time in the wilderness. God had transformed them and given them a new way to live. They were equipped and ready for the challenges that were ahead. The journey from Egypt, and through the wilderness, difficult and arduous as it was, also helped them become the people they needed to be to start the life that God had in store for them. Their journey wasn't over, but it had progressed. Something significant changed as they crossed from the wilderness to the new land. They were no longer slaves, or the children of slaves, but they were now chosen people, God's own people. Everything, from their identity to their purpose to their future vision, had undergone a transition in the wilderness.

The rest of the Bible is largely a continuation of Israel becoming God's people. It is a continuation of this journey.

In fact, if you keep reading, the people continue a cycle of falling back into sin (something the Bible describes as "slavery"); they cry out to God, those prayers are answered, God forgives them, and God leads them out of their sin and toward a new future complete with a wilderness time in between.

The Old Testament begins with the exodus and eventually moves to a companion story: the Babylonian exile. Nearly a thousand years after the people entered the new land, ready to be God's chosen people, they found themselves in the wilderness again. They had grown unfaithful. They forgot their purpose and mission. They sometimes tolerated, or even worshipped, idols. They no longer remembered the promises God made to them and the ones they made back to God. They had lost the instructions and law, the companion guide for the new life God had called them to live. So they had to embark on a new journey, not one of their own choosing. They were conquered by the Babylonians and dragged into exile in a foreign land (what today is southern Iraq). After nearly sixty years, the next generation of Israelites, most of whom had only known Babylon as their home, were able to leave that place, return to Jerusalem, and rebuild. These two narratives, the exodus and the exile, bookend the Hebrew scriptures, and they are the model for countless journeys that individual people of faith have gone through: leaving "home," wandering in the wilderness, and entering a new reality complete with a new beginning.

The Bible is a story of many journeys but also one big journey. It is no surprise that, when Jesus came to save all people, the scriptures described his life and death as an "exodus." Just as the Passover lamb was used to mark the doorways of those who would be saved from Pharaoh and led out of Egypt, so Jesus was the Lamb of God who would die to save all people. (Matthew's Gospel makes a point of drawing parallels between Jesus and Moses. Jesus's family had gone to Egypt, just as Moses did. Moses brought down God's law from the mountain; Jesus taught about God's law in a sermon on a mount. Moses helped deliver the Israelites from slavery; Jesus liberated the people from the bondage of sin. Matthew wants us not to miss this.)

As Jesus's followers, we live this life as a time of wandering in the wilderness, one foot in this world and one foot in the world to come. Through Jesus's resurrection we look forward to a new reality and a promised land, the new heaven and new earth that scripture envisions. It is the exodus story, except this time the journey is permanent, the destination is free of suffering and challenges, and the invitation is to all people. It is this overarching story that we are a part of.

God is freeing you from everything that holds you back from experiencing the life God created you for. God is removing chains, conquering fear, forgiving sins, and restoring an authentic sense of who you really are. God is leading you through a wilderness period, that time and space in between here and there. In the wilderness God is refining you, teaching you, reshaping you, and leading you. Finally, God will deliver you to a new "land," a new place in life full of new possibilities and potential. Just as in scripture, that is the overarching story of our whole life, but within that there are all sorts of little journeys.

In your career you may follow this arc, several times maybe, in the course of your work life. When it comes to relationships, we will retravel this story several times over the course of our lives. When we are faced with a life change, the loss of someone we love, or a setback that changes everything about our life, we will travel this wilderness road. Anytime we make a transition, from high school to college, from school to work, from work to retirement, from singleness to marriage, from being a kid to being a parent, we will travel the wilderness road. Whatever the change, we will find ourselves retracing the steps—leaving something old behind, entering an unknown wilderness, and finally arriving at a new place. Along the way, we will become new people. In each instance of change in our life, we have the gift and opportunity to become someone new, to grow more into the person God calls us to be.

Because of all the change in the course of one life, and because life isn't linear, you will at various times find yourself in all three stages. You may get to the new reality and find that you start the journey all over. You might be in the promised land in your career, while you feel lost in the wilderness at home. Some of your journeys will end in a remarkable and beautiful way, while some changes may never fully come to fruition. As with Moses, there may be certain aspects of your life that you never fully realize on this side of heaven.

Regardless, I want you to know that the journey is

worth it. It is worth having the courage to take that risk, make that change, step out from that safe place, and set out for a new reality that you cannot yet see. It is worth wading into that deep water, with the trust that it will part before you, or trekking across the wilderness, without the certainty of how long you might have to be there. It is worth it, not only because there is a destination to which God is leading you but also because the journey itself makes you into the person God created you to be. I think that last point is so important to remember. This side of heaven, we don't always reach all the destinations we set out for. But it is the journey that actually is the agent for our change. God uses the journey to create and re-create us. In so many ways, the destination is the journey, at least in this life.

Since I have talked about my own journey in many places, let me finish it, or at least tell you where I am on the road. God brought me through some of the most difficult wilderness experiences of my life. Now, for twelve years, I have had the incredible honor of pastoring a church that has grown far more than I ever dreamed possible. Each year my church has one big Easter service, during which all of our sites from around the city gather in one huge theatre to worship. Last year, I walked out on stage and looked up to more people than I had ever seen gathered at our church. It numbered in the thousands. But what is important about that isn't the number but something else. As I stood there ready to preach, it occurred to me just how faithful God has been, and just how much God has brought me through. I don't think I am done, not even close. And I bet there are some challenges up ahead that will require new trust and new growth. But the sight was incredible as I stood there. And as I write, I think about all that I would have missed if I didn't trust God for this journey. On my own, my life would have been much smaller, much safer, much less interesting. God has taken me to places and given me work that is far greater than anything I could have asked for or imagined. I know the journey isn't over, and I am not in a rush anymore. I am not in a big hurry to "get somewhere." I realize that the journey alone is worth it. In so many ways, it is the destination.

We will never fully escape the fears that can seize us or slow us down. The disciples regularly were faced with fears new and old. We will face them as well. But with God's help, we can learn to be less defined and constricted by our fears. Maybe this side of heaven we will never stop being afraid, at least not completely. But we can no longer allow our fears to guide us. Instead we will learn to take courage, to be bold, and to trust in God's leadership. Fears may still be a reality, but they no longer hold so much power over us. That is a gift of traveling on this journey long enough. We learn to better differentiate the authentic voice of God and the deceptive lies of fear.

Finally, and most important, the journey teaches us that God is never far away from us. The good news is that you are never alone. That might sound trite to some of you, but I assure you that there is power in knowing you are not alone. Think about it.

When they were younger, none of my three kids ever

wanted to go into the basement, especially my daughter Carly. She was so scared to go down there. There could be monsters or robbers or the creature from the scary movie she just watched. But if her younger brother George would go with her, if she could just have someone else right by her side, she would go into the basement. I always thought this was funny; if there really was a monster, I don't think her five-year-old younger brother would have been much help. But that didn't matter. There is power and courage that come simply from knowing you are not alone.

If you are a grown person, maybe you have trouble connecting with that. Well, consider this. In 1973, upon his release and the release of his fellow soldiers from Vietnam, Admiral James Stockdale and his crew of POWs made headlines. They had spent time as prisoners in a brutal place that came to be known sarcastically as the Hanoi Hilton. Because of their resistance, eleven of them were isolated in three-by-nine cages and tortured. They were the longest held prisoners of war in American history, yet they had a surprisingly high rate of survival and continued service. The other prisoners credited the admiral. During their imprisonment, he continued to secretly lead them, devising ways to deal with torture and creating benchmarks in order to survive. The most important thing Admiral Stockdale instituted in the prison was a secret way to communicate through tapping. This tap code, as it came to be known, combatted the single most dangerous part of imprisonment—isolation. The code simply let each prisoner know: "You are not alone." Knowing they were not alone saved their lives. There is power in knowing you are not alone.

I have a lot of pastoral conversations with people struggling or going through a crisis. Maybe it is addiction, grief, a broken marriage, or parenting trouble. I wish in those situations that I had magic words, some kind of silver bullet that would make everything better. But usually the best I can do is say, "Have you met so-and-so? Let me connect you. They have gone through something similar." When we can connect with someone else who has been where we are, it lightens our load just a bit and introduces some amount of hope. Why? Because you realize you are not alone. There is power in knowing you are not alone.

That is the word God sent to the people through the prophet Isaiah during their time in exile in Babylon, and it is the word that God still means for us to hear today during our most trying times:

> When you pass through the waters, I will be
> with you;
>   and through the rivers, they shall not
>   overwhelm you;
> . . . .
> Fear not, for I am with you.
> (Isaiah 43:2, 5 ESV)

Perhaps that is why at the birth of Jesus they gave him the name Emanuel, or God with Us. Maybe that is why his last words on earth were, "Remember I am with you always, even to the end of the age." There is power in knowing you are not alone. If the journey teaches us anything, it is that God is always with us, always working for our good, never leaving or forsaking us. So take courage. You can risk the bold step, the uncertain path, or the crazy call on your life. You can do it. Go for it. Trust me. You got this.

ACKNOWLEDGMENTS

———

I n some ways, this book has been two decades in the making. Pastoral ministry is an adventure in navigating change and learning how to face transitions. Throw in a family, three kids, a dog, and a growing church and my own life has been a case study in why this book is so important. The truth is I wrote the book for myself because I wish I would have had it earlier. I know that I will continue to need it in the future. But, what I have discovered from talking with others is that all of us are constantly trying to chart a course through some sort of transition. Whether it is leaving a job or starting a new one, having a baby or losing a loved one, managing the chaos of a family or the solitude of being alone, we are constantly transitioning.

I want to thank all of the people who made this project possible and encouraged me to write the book despite my apprehensiveness. I'm grateful to my coworker Denee Bowers at The Gathering for planting the seed for this book. I am grateful to Susan Salley at Abingdon Press, who has always encouraged me and been a cheerleader for what I wanted to say. Her affirmation and guidance were invaluable to me. My editor Randy Horick stayed on me weekly and helped clarify and sharpen my ideas. I owe an ongoing debt of gratitude to my assistant Amy Sanders without whom nothing on my to-do list would get done. I am fortunate to work alongside an amazing staff and with an incredible church at The Gathering. The community and support I gain from being their pastor sustains me for the work I do. The Gathering has been one long lesson in the excitement change can bring and the importance of managing those transitions with care, intentionality, and faith. I also want to acknowledge with gratitude the work of William Bridges and his book *Managing Transitions*, a classic in the business world that first sparked my imagination about how a similar idea could apply to our personal lives.

Finally, I want to recognize, thank, and celebrate my family. My wife, Jessica, has taught me more about my faith than anyone else in my life. Without her, my ministry would not be possible. And to my three kids, Caleb, Carly, and George: you inspire me to be a better pastor. I love you and am grateful for the ways you support me and for all that you give up so that I can minister to others. For all the ways this book may help others navigate a difficult and challenging time in their life, thanks be to God who is always with us.

Matt Miofsky
March 8, 2019